CRITICAL CONVERSATIONS *in* CO-TEACHING

A Problem-Solving Approach

Carrie Chapman

Cate Hart Hyatt

Solution Tree | Press
a division of
Solution Tree

555 North Morton Street
Bloomington, IN 47404

800.733.6786 (toll free) / 812.336.7700
FAX: 812.336.7790

email: info@solution-tree.com
solution-tree.com

Visit **go.solution-tree.com/specialneeds** to download the reproducibles in this book.
Printed in the United States of America

15 14 13 12   2 3 4 5

Library of Congress Cataloging-in-Publication Data
Chapman, Carrie.
  Critical conversations in co-teaching : a problem-solving approach / Carrie Chapman. Cate Hart Hyatt.
    p. cm.
  Includes bibliographical references and index.
  ISBN 978-1-935542-32-2 (perfect bound) -- ISBN 978-1-935542-33-9 (library edition) 1. Teaching teams. 2. Individualized instruction. I. Hyatt, Cate Hart, II. Title.
  LB1029.T4C43 2011
  371.14'8--dc23
                              2011017866

Solution Tree
Jeffrey C. Jones, CEO & President

Solution Tree Press
President: Douglas M. Rife
Publisher: Robert D. Clouse
Vice President of Production: Gretchen Knapp
Managing Production Editor: Caroline Wise
Senior Production Editor: Suzanne Kraszewski
Copy Editor: Rachel Rosolina
Proofreader: Elisabeth Abrams
Cover and Text Designer: Orlando Angel

ACKNOWLEDGMENTS

We would like to thank three families for supporting us throughout this process. First, we want to thank our colleagues at the Center on Education and Lifelong Learning (CELL), Indiana Institute on Disability and Community, Indiana University, and the hundreds of collaborative partners with whom we have had the grand pleasure of working over the past decade. We are constantly inspired by our CELL mates and especially to our director for many years, Sandi Cole, who has allowed us to follow our hearts and focus much of our work in the areas of collaboration and co-teaching. A special thanks to our colleague James Robinson, whose commitment to improving instructional matches for all students helped inform our work. Thanks also to Kay Moore, who has continued to provide her clerical magic as we write, revise, and develop new materials.

Secondly, we would like to show our appreciation to the supportive and ever-growing Solution Tree family. We especially want to thank Claudia Wheatley and Gretchen Knapp for proposing that we bring our work to a larger audience and to Suzanne Kraszewski, our editor extraordinaire, for patiently shepherding us through this process.

And last but not least, we would be remiss without showing gratitude to our own families: our husbands Dave Chapman and Bob Hyatt, our children, and our ever-growing grandchildren (in number and spirit) who have provided wonderful distractions along the way, but always with enthusiasm and encouragement for us to get back on track and finish strong.

Solution Tree Press would like to thank the following reviewers:

Patricia Alvarez-McHatton
Assistant Professor, Department of Special
  Education
University of South Florida
Tampa, Florida

Patricia Kohler-Evans
Associate Professor, Department of Early
  Childhood and Special Education
University of Central Arkansas
Conway, Arkansas

Wendy Weichel Murawski
Assistant Professor, Department of Special
   Education
California State University—Northridge
Northridge, California

Ann Nevin
Professor Emerita
Arizona State University
Tempe, Arizona

Emily Sims
English, Journalism Teacher
Orchard Farm High School
St. Charles, Missouri

Jacqueline S. Thousand
Professor, Department of Special Education
California State University—San Marcos
San Marcos, California

Visit **go.solution-tree.com/specialneeds** to download the reproducibles in this book.

TABLE OF CONTENTS

ABOUT THE AUTHORS

Carrie Chapman, PhD, is an assistant professor of education at Minnesota State University, Mankato, where she is also the co-teaching coordinator for the College of Education. After serving as a public school educator and coach for twelve years, she earned her doctoral degree from Indiana University in curriculum and instruction with an emphasis in special education. She then worked as a faculty member at IU and as a research associate in the Center on Education and Lifelong Learning (CELL) at the Indiana Institute on Disability and Community located at Indiana University. Dr. Chapman's primary area of expertise is in the development of co-teaching, collaboration, and consultation strategies with educators who are focused on improving the teaching-learning process for *all* students. She has worked side by side with diverse educator groups in public and private schools throughout the Midwest who are committed to helping each student, regardless of his or her circumstances, develop and learn as effectively and efficiently as possible. Although Dr. Chapman has enjoyed a great deal of success as a grant writer, author, and presenter, she is most at home in the local schools working with teachers, student teachers, and students.

Cate Hart Hyatt, MS, has spent more than thirty years as an educator, preschool through graduate school. She currently delivers a variety of effective professional development strategies, trainings, graduate courses, and onsite coaching as a collaborative team member at CELL, Indiana Institute on Disability and Community, Indiana University. She shares CELL's mission to work with schools and communities to welcome, include, educate, and support all learners while providing quality professional development to increase organizational and individual capacity in K–12 schools.

In addition, Cate led Indiana's efforts in VETS: Voicing Experiences Through Service. VETS was funded with a $1.3 million grant from the

Corporation for National and Community Service in partnership with colleagues in Maryland and Vermont to expand service opportunities as part of transition planning for youth with disabilities (ages 14–21) and increase their participation in service, specifically through the gathering of oral histories for the National Veterans History Project. She is currently contracted by the Indiana Department of Education to provide technical assistance for Learn and Serve Indiana school districts. In addition, she regularly teaches a service learning course for Indiana University students.

INTRODUCTION

First and foremost, we are teachers. We have each spent more than thirty years as educators in preschool through graduate school classrooms. As partners at the Center on Education and Lifelong Learning at Indiana University, Bloomington, for a dozen years, we have trained nearly three thousand educators throughout the Midwest in the art of shared practice in individual, school, and districtwide settings. During that time, we implemented a variety of effective professional development strategies, training and onsite coaching opportunities, and graduate courses to foster better collaboration, co-teaching, and teaming among our colleagues and students.

Regardless of whether we are co-teaching together, consulting with school districts, preparing pre-service teachers, or working on other favorite passions, we both try to embed quality professional learning opportunities into every conversation we have with other educators.

As we examined the partnerships of educators with whom we have worked, we found that the secret to quality co-teaching is not so much the strategies or models the teachers were implementing, but rather the kinds of conversations they engaged in. These conversations were what ultimately determined their success in working together.

Many of the stories we have collected during our work appear in this book, and they are what has convinced us of the power of critical conversations.

- Sarah Beth felt that her students with learning disabilities had been ousted from their self-contained room to be spread out all over the middle school—surely to fail. How would she be able to work with different teachers every period?

- Barry always helped his freshman algebra students by modifying and adapting his lessons for struggling students. How could he be positive about his co-teacher, Wilma, who mostly milled around, often reading the newspaper or checking her email during class?

- Alex and Maya, the speech pathologist and the English teacher, wanted to co-teach as a way to finally be seen as valued colleagues. How could they use their skills and knowledge more effectively by supporting the primary-level teachers?

In all of these situations, teachers found ways to work together to add value for their students through co-teaching.

Co-teaching is most frequently used to provide access and targeted support to students with disabilities, ensuring they have access to a rigorous general education curriculum in a least restrictive environment. Benefits of collaborative partnerships include common goals, shared resources, shared responsibility, and accountability for all students. The benefits of co-teaching have expanded to include support for students with higher abilities, students with speech difficulties, and also English learners (ELs). More recently, we are seeing whole teams of co-teachers (general educators, special educators, speech therapists, Title I teachers, and EL educators) all working together, as well as university-based student teachers co-teaching with their cooperating teachers at school sites.

In addition to the benefits for students, collaborative conversations help teachers. We know that students improve when educators improve, and that problems are best solved when teachers collaborate and learn together. This collaboration paired with strong leadership allows teachers to achieve ambitious goals for their students.

The Elementary and Secondary Education Act as reauthorized by the No Child Left Behind Act of 2001 states that professional development needs to directly impact a teacher's classroom practices and student achievement. Realizing this, several other major educational organizations have recently united to adopt a new definition of professional learning that taps the expertise of the educators in the school and at the district office.

This new definition describes professional development as a comprehensive, sustained, and intensive approach to improving teachers' and principals' effectiveness in raising student achievement, and fosters collective responsibility for improved student performance, while aligning with rigorous state academic achievement standards for students as well as related local educational agency and school improvement goals. Key implications are that professional learning is conducted among educators at the school and facilitated by well-prepared school principals and school-based professional development coaches, mentors, master teachers, or other teacher leaders, and that it occurs several times per week among established teams of teachers, principals, and other instructional staff members who are engaged in a continuous cycle of improvement.

In line with this new definition, Learning Forward, a favorite professional organization of ours, recently adopted as its purpose: "*Every educator engages in effective professional learning every day so every student achieves*" (www.learningforward.org). This same purpose has become a rallying point for most major educational organizations nationally, and it also aligns perfectly with the kinds of conversations you will find in this book.

Critical Conversations in Co-Teaching: A Problem-Solving Approach is a practitioner's guide to understanding and establishing a variety of co-teaching models; it is for the Sarah Beths, Barrys, Wilmas, Mayas, and Alexes who want to reach and teach *all* students, better. Our approach offers four sets of conversation prompts and protocols designed to foster dramatic improvements in the way you communicate with colleagues. These conversations have paved the way for more effective and efficient shared teaching practices for hundreds of teachers, and they can help you create a truly value-added collaborative practice.

To be honest, when we first began our work many years ago, we didn't think much about how co-teaching added to the value of classrooms. We knew the practice helped get students with disabilities into classrooms where they could have access to the general education curriculum. We also knew that we really liked to work together and our students seemed to thrive—especially the ones who typically struggled.

Then we conducted a series of presentations for a principal—Mr. Jenkins—and his faculty. Five of his teachers (four freshman English teachers and a special educator) had attended one of our earliest trainings and convinced him to let them give co-teaching a try. They saw benefits immediately, and the only thing he did to support them was to provide help scheduling students. Observations in these rooms were a delight; he watched highly engaged students, theatrical teachers portraying literary characters, and enlivened classes. In fact, he noted that these partnerships seemed to take on lives of their own.

He began to wonder if the qualitative data were enough to show a good return on investment. He recognized that these co-teachers were some of the most effective teachers he had. He wondered, "Were students getting the same product or service with individual teachers, or were they getting more bang for the buck when these teachers co-taught?" He saw the soft measures—happy teachers, more engaged students, increased social interactions for students with disabilities; these were apparent to him from casual conversations with his co-teachers and his occasional observations in their classrooms.

The hard measures were, well, harder to measure. He reviewed test scores for the past four years. For all the good he had observed, the students in co-taught classes had fared no better on typical tests. He thought, "If I am paying at least $100,000 for my fifth-period freshman English class because I have two highly qualified and experienced teachers in a room with an average size class, I want to make sure I am getting my money's worth."

After an agonizing examination of their shared practices, the group realized none of their partner configurations had done enough to provide their students with a more efficient or more effective learning experience. In fact, they came to see that each of their pairs was actually doing no more than what one really great teacher would do—even when two great teachers were in the room.

The first thing they did to rectify this was to brainstorm a list of nonexamples—what their co-teaching looked like when it did *not* add value. They were surprised at just how quickly the list grew (see table I.1).

Table I.1: Value-Added Nonexamples

Content Teacher Actions	Special Educator Actions
Provides review of upcoming unit test for whole class	Taps students on the shoulder to wake up or keep place in the text
Proctors a test to small group of advanced students	Assigns seat work for large group with little facilitation or assistance offered
Takes attendance, checks homework, passes out papers, performs crowd control	Presents PowerPoint presentation of new material
Takes half of group to computer lab	Keeps other half in classroom waiting their turn, monitors homework

At first, listing nonexamples seemed like an absurd activity to the teachers, but it helped them realize just how easy it is to waste valuable resources for little payoff. Wanting to be better stewards of the financial resources of their district, they became much more intentional about showing value for their collaborative efforts. They proved that 1 + 1 = more than 2.

Our book provides a framework for adding value to teaching and learning through collaborative practice. After you and your partner conduct your own critical conversations in co-teaching, you will be able to clearly identify what strengths each of you bring to the table. You will also be able to explain the investment that your time, talent, and experience offers, and hopefully you will be able to see measurable returns on that investment.

When we set out to write *Critical Conversations in Co-Teaching*, we researched the existing literature. There are a number of available academic books related to collaboration and co-teaching, and many use models to enhance instruction. Some emphasize the importance of building a relationship, but none offer a process to help build collaborative relationships—the first step in building a quality collaborative practice. While professional development books focus on communication skills, not a single book even remotely offered a specific focus on conversations for co-teaching.

Educators constantly remind us that they want practical examples and stories about teachers that show how co-teaching strategies really make a positive difference for students. They do not want academic jargon, irrelevant research, or impossible instructions. We reviewed textbooks, journal articles, web resources, and professional development offerings in our quest to provide examples of best practices and common pitfalls, but the real experts—the ones we learned the most from—are the practicing teachers with whom we have had the privilege to work. Their conversations continue to guide our thinking and our work. The case studies in this book are compilations of real-life stories. The authentic conversations we describe come from their experiences, and they bring our framework to life.

By using the framework, prompts, and protocols in this book, you and your colleagues will be able to address not only what co-teaching strategies you might use, but *how* you will implement them to build on the strengths each of you bring to the classroom you share. The conversations will facilitate discussions and aid your partnerships through the continual questioning and challenging of one another in your search to reach all of your students. Having critical conversations can transform the way you plan and teach together, perhaps helping you reconnect with the passion you had when you first decided you wanted to teach.

Together we have more than thirty years of experience training educators across many disciplines. We have successfully coached general educators, special educators, and other school personnel who are now using these critical conversations to guide their work. Our framework is designed to enhance your shared practice using a simple structure and process of talking together. It can create profound differences in the way you work together and in the outcomes you can expect from the young people whose futures you help shape. We have seen it transform our colleagues and the schools in which we work. It has become our passion in education. We invite you to join our conversation.

Book Organization and Design

Chapters 1 through 9 begin with conversation starters that focus on the main points of each chapter. We hope these guiding questions will provoke conversation, initiate problem solving, expand your thinking to new possibilities, and help deepen your views. The conversation starters are designed to help you examine those beliefs, values, and practices that can enrich your partnership, come up with great solutions to vexing problems, create amazing possibilities, and add value to your teaching.

You'll no doubt want to reflect individually on each conversation starter before mapping out a plan with your partner. There are no right answers for conversation starters, just the answers that you and your partner decide are right. You may have multiple teaching partners. Each partnership is unique, requiring that you tackle different conversation starters and different protocols with each of your colleagues. And remember, nobody wins if someone loses. Hopefully even in your disagreements, you can find a working solution. Good partners learn the fine art of compromise. It's easier to compromise when you remember the goal is to add value for your students.

Chapter Descriptions

Chapter 1, "An Opening Invitation to Co-Teaching Conversations," outlines the key elements of co-teaching and the structure of the critical conversations framework presented later in the book. It explores the rationale for co-teaching and provides examples from real schools.

In chapter 2, "Co-Teaching Models," you will learn a variety of ways in which you and your co-teaching partners can structure and focus your instruction. We provide a structure for different types of models and their organization, detailed explanations for each model, the assets and challenges of using particular models, and examples of why and when co-teachers choose to use a particular model.

Chapter 3, "The Critical Conversations in Co-Teaching Framework," explains the structure of our approach to co-teaching. More specifically, *critical conversations* are sets of conversation protocols—detailed activity plans for communication and reflection—that span the wide spectrum of exchanges that effective collaborators experience. The critical conversations protocols begin with a focus on relationship building and end by helping you and your partner ensure the necessary system supports are in place so that you can continue to grow and improve in your collaborative practice.

Chapter 4, "Critical Conversations in Action," offers a preview of the four sets of critical conversations and the protocols for each set. The keys to beginning a quality co-teaching practice include participating in these value-added conversations, which engage our co-teaching partners, examine student data, and work to enhance instruction. The chapter also provides stories from teachers just like you who illustrate the framework in action.

Chapter 5, "Expanding Co-Teaching Conversations," investigates set 4 in greater detail. It explores what happens once partners and teams have established critical conversations and co-teachers and administrators wish to spread the wealth to other colleagues in a more systemic approach to the implementation of co-teaching. This chapter will guide you toward this larger goal. The rationale and important definitions within this process are highlighted in the text that follows.

The next four chapters provide the heart of our process, the actual protocols you can use to develop your partnership. Each of these chapters—chapter 6, "Critical Conversations Protocols: Set 1—Engage Partners"; chapter 7, "Critical Conversations Protocols: Set 2—Examine Data"; chapter 8, "Critical Conversations Protocols: Set 3—Enhance Instruction"; and chapter 9, "Critical Conversations Protocols: Set 4—Expand Impact"—begins with focus questions and anticipated outcomes and contains three types of conversations: (1) non-negotiable, (2) special occasion, and (3) in a perfect world.

In conclusion, we hope you are sufficiently curious about the prospects of improving the learning opportunities not only for your students but also for you and your colleagues. Now we invite you to join the conversation.

AN OPENING INVITATION TO CO-TEACHING CONVERSATIONS

1

Conversation Starters

- In what ways can you and your colleagues collaborate to more effectively meet the increasingly complex needs of today's students?
- What are the key elements of co-teaching that address your needs and the needs of your students?
- What critical decision-making factors influence your decisions about co-teaching?

The challenges we face in today's schools demand ever-increasing creativity and insightfulness from teachers and administrators committed to improving the learning environment for students. Educators must meet more and more demands from administration and the public, and they must address an array of federal and state mandates, such as the Individuals With Disabilities Education Act and No Child Left Behind, which directly address issues of student access to the general education curriculum, assessment, and instructional accountability for all teachers and schools. Additionally, classrooms truly mirror our larger world with their increasing diversity in student and family backgrounds and wide variety of student learning styles. Educators are always trying to find ways to better serve their students, families, and the community. The skills necessary to achieve these increased demands within the classroom will most often incorporate various forms of collaboration and an ever wider range of teaching methods (Bronson & Dentith, 2005; Preddy, 2008).

There are specific realities that lead schools, teachers, family members, and other interested parties to engage more purposefully with each other. Review the following list, and identify the key realities you and your school need to be aware of in order to plan and design learning together:

- Increasing diversity in student culture, ethnicity, socioeconomic reality, and language

- More varied student learning styles
- Curricular access for all students as required by educational mandates and the resultant compulsory local and state assessments
- Increasing student and family involvement with community agencies for support services
- Increasing curriculum requirements
- The implementation of federal and state mandates for highly qualified teacher status
- The implementation of response to intervention (RTI) requirements of special education law through teacher teams
- Increasing decision making about curriculum, assessment, and evaluation protocols by interdisciplinary teams
- Increasing questions posed to schools from lawmakers, administrators, and other stakeholders about accountability and a return on the expense of their educational investment

If you were able to identify even a few items in the list, you are similar to most schools and teachers today. From a logistical standpoint, individual teachers typically cannot provide everything students need; only in a very few exceptional cases do we see an extraordinary teacher who comes close. Collectively, the adults in a school have a much better chance of meeting student (and adult) needs through collaborative work: planning, designing, implementation, and evaluation of results. In addition, collaborative teacher practices may provide increased opportunities for improving the academic gains of all students (Cole, Waldron, & Majd, 2004). Co-teaching is an instructional model that can serve as a means to better meet the increasing demands on schools to improve student achievement.

Key Elements in Co-Teaching

Some of the earliest descriptors of *co-teaching* come from the work of Bauwens, Hourcade, and Friend (1989) and Cook and Friend (1995); the definition often cited is "two or more professionals delivering substantive instruction to a diverse or blended group of students in a single physical space" (Cook & Friend, 1995, p. 2). This definition of co-teaching has evolved from a general education–special education strategy to one of good practice for all schooling. As the practice of co-teaching and the realities of schools have further developed and evolved, we now see the definition of co-teaching as being more inclusive and holistic. The definition of co-teaching has further evolved for us as we have developed our framework:

> *Co-teaching* is an effective, evidence-based instructional strategy in which two or more caring professionals share responsibility for a group of students and work collaboratively to add instructional value to enhance their efforts.

For teachers to truly work together as quality co-teachers, they must gain a complete understanding of the three components involved in this teaching option. These components are the key factors educators consider when making decisions:

1 The students for whom they are responsible
2 The adults—the partners—with whom joint teaching is done
3 The professional practices in which they engage (curriculum, instruction, assessment, and classroom culture)

The Students

As simplistic as it may sound, knowing as much as possible about your students is essential for sound decision making. Typically, we find that this is an easier task in elementary schools, where students stay in the same classroom or have the same teacher for multiple subjects or parts of the school day. At the middle or high school levels, course content becomes the organizational structure; teachers tend to teach only one or a few subjects, with multiple groups of students rotating through each classroom. Secondary level teachers may have as many as five to six class periods a day with twenty to thirty or more students per class—a very large number of students to try and get to know. Even with those challenges, all teachers need to work intensely to find out as much about their students as possible to enhance the total learning environment.

Two teachers working together in a co-taught classroom can make gaining knowledge about students' learning styles, academic assets and challenges, and personal traits easier and more efficient. Each teacher can be responsible for more fully understanding targeted groups of students (for example, students in special education or English learners), or the teachers can decide how they might relate more effectively with different students. Combining their efforts by sharing data, observations, and preferences, they can gain a more complete picture of each student in their class. They can then use this information to enhance their planning, implementation, and evaluation of lessons and coursework. Clearly it allows for more effective differentiation of instruction, a more thoughtful grouping of students, and it moves teachers away from the one-size-fits-all mentality. Teachers who have a more complete knowledge of their students can then use it to supplement and enhance the academic content in any class.

The Adults

We cannot overstate the importance of teachers clarifying their own values, assumptions, and educational goals, and then following up with meaningful conversations with their partners. Self-knowledge goes a long way in making the co-teaching partnership grow and develop in healthy ways for both teachers and students. Each teacher must know and be able to articulate his or her beliefs and philosophy of teaching and learning in a way that leads to a shared vision of the co-teaching work—because teaching together makes what was once a private practice now a very public one. Co-teachers must then have conversations with each other on a wide variety of personal and professional topics, so that they can learn about each other and work to become equal partners (Bouck, 2007). This parity of roles within the teaching partnership is crucial to effective co-teaching, as is the teachers' personal and professional compatibility (Kohler-Evans, 2006; Rice & Zigmond, 2000; Salend, Gordon, & Lopez-Vona, 2002).

Developing a compatible joint teaching style and choosing instructional strategies and co-teaching models will depend on each teacher's self-knowledge, the individual attributes each teacher brings to the co-teaching classroom, and the meshing together of co-teachers' individual styles, preferences, expertise, and interests. Without deep and continuing conversations, teachers will be unable to move through the developmental stages of the framework, and their work together and with students will be diminished.

The Professional Practices

Each co-teaching partnership has its own professional practice. The activities teachers engage in within their classrooms are the teaching practices that will determine student learning. Co-teachers negotiate explicitly understood agreements with each other on what their joint teaching looks like, and many factors impact this professional practice. Of primary importance is quality interpersonal communication. Additional issues that impact teaching practice and continually mesh with the content and process of professional practice include the physical arrangement of the classroom, content knowledge and planning, curriculum goals, adaptations and modifications to the content or learning activities, instructional presentation, classroom management, and learning assessment (Gately & Gately, 2001). Both the tangible evidence of collaboration (concrete materials developed for co-teaching) and the intangible evidence (the collaborative personal skills needed to co-teach) are also important elements to acknowledge within the co-teaching experience. All of these are important considerations for co-teachers to agree upon prior to beginning their work together and to review regularly as they develop their practice together.

Teaching is a complex process made even more demanding when two professionals perform that work in concert. When all decisions in the co-teaching process take students, adults, and professional practice into account, co-teachers will find the best ways to teach coherently for students to learn.

A Shared Understanding

Each teacher should develop his or her own understanding of the individual elements, but more importantly, the co-teaching partnership must also come to a shared understanding of each component so practice is truly blended into a value-added shared practice. By *value-added*, we mean that co-teaching partnerships must determine how they can provide the most effective *and* efficient support for students in ways that would never be possible with one teacher alone. It is in this way that co-teachers truly add value to the teaching and learning process. As each co-teaching partnership develops, other considerations come into play, and this shared understanding is critical to the co-teachers' continued success.

Each section of this book will continually revisit these three key co-teaching factors (students, adults, and professional practice), along with four sets of critical conversations in our value-added co-teaching framework. These combine to provide the necessary comprehensive developmental structure to help you and your partners build your quality co-teaching practice. The value-added co-teaching framework begins simply: *we talk to one another.*

The Four Critical Conversations

Four sets of critical conversations will provide opportunities for some of the best professional development you and your partner can experience without leaving your building. As you intentionally focus on building your adult relationship and target your students in more meaningful ways, you will find your professional practice improving in ways that lead not only to greater student achievement, but to a feeling of more connectedness to your profession. Many teachers who have used this framework report that the process re-energized them and reminded them of why they became educators to begin with.

The critical conversations in this book are designed to lead you and your partners through the framework. They are developmental in nature—they follow a path that partners tend to move through as they begin and then become more collaborative in their work together. The four sets of critical conversations and their main goals are as follows:

1 **Engage Partners**—In these conversations, partners establish a shared vision, establish the partnership, and lay the collaborative foundation.

2 **Examine Data**—In these conversations, partners focus on results, use data about students to make instructional improvements, and dig into the data.

3 **Enhance Instruction**—In these conversations, partners add value, using the partnership to teach together and make more impact than one teacher could do alone.

4 **Expand Impact**—In these conversations, partners take a systems view toward improving instruction, and they sustain their effort.

Each set of critical conversations is made up of specific protocols—discussion plans and activities to work through with your partner or team. These protocols fit into three categories—non-negotiable conversations (recommended for all partners), special occasion protocols (to use in specific situations), and "in a perfect world" protocols (to use as enrichment activities to extend learning). Each set of critical conversations, while not absolutely necessary for co-teaching to take place, will go a long way toward ensuring that professional practices improve learning and all professionals involved are sharing their knowledge, skills, and talents to the benefit of all students. For now, we briefly introduce each of the factors you will need to consider when choosing a co-teaching model and deciding which conversations to have.

Like most teachers, we started our own journeys in co-teaching looking for that silver bullet to give us the answers. Even now, most schools we visit ask for various models and specific strategies to get them started. We provide examples of various models and instructional strategies to enhance co-teaching, but only after presenting them within a comprehensive framework. In this guide, we present co-teaching models in chapter 2 and encourage you to learn about the models, but we remind you that the real collaborative work begins in chapter 3 as you learn about the critical conversations that will lay the foundation for successfully working together.

Rationale for Co-Teaching

Much of the emphasis and research examining co-teaching as a viable option for supporting student learning has come from the realm of special education (Murawski & Swanson, 2001). This work has focused primarily on how co-teachers work to assist students with mild to moderate disabilities in the general education curriculum. Other research that has examined co-teaching as an option in schools (Bartholomay, Wallace, & Mason, 2001; Bronson & Dentith, 2005; King, 2003; York-Barr, Ghere, & Sommerness, 2007) has additionally focused on general educators working together with a variety of other school professionals in various structural and curricular arrangements to create supportive learning environments within collaborative schools. Using school reform and research-based practices for all students has played a part in many closely related areas of the research literature. Those areas most relevant to daily classroom practice in the quality implementation by co-teachers include professional learning communities (PLCs), response to intervention (RTI), differentiated instruction (DI), and universal design for learning (UDL). A brief introduction to each of these follows, in which we include our own observations and real-life examples from schools. Future chapters will utilize concepts from these areas in furthering insights about how to implement co-teaching as a useful instructional strategy to enhance each of these districtwide initiatives.

Professional Learning Communities

Becoming a professional learning community is important as schools and educators progress toward a more effective learning environment for students and adults alike (DuFour, DuFour, Eaker, &

Karhanek, 2004; DuFour & Eaker, 1998). DuFour, DuFour, Eaker, and Many (2010) describe a PLC as "composed of collaborative teams whose members work interdependently to achieve common goals. . . linked to the purpose of learning for all" (p. 3). One of the most salient characteristics of the PLC concept is the emphasis on collaborative teams and the varied work they do together in schools to focus on improved student achievement. A natural outgrowth of collaborative teams in schools is the closer relationship among colleagues and improved student instruction that comes from co-teaching. Co-teachers working together in classrooms, as part of collaborative teams, can also engage in collective inquiry as well as action orientation and experimentation—two additional characteristics of PLCs.

Work in PLCs moves what has been a singular, isolated practice in the culture of schools into a collaborative culture where teachers' best professional development, learning, and teaching improvement can come from each other (DuFour et al., 2010; Schmoker, 2010). Working as a co-teacher can become the ultimate work in a PLC—the close, collaborative teaching of partners engaged in learning with students and each other.

Miller County Middle School: Interdisciplinary Teams

In a Miller County middle school where the faculty has already been engaged in PLC work, interdisciplinary teams (including special and general educators) have been co-planning instructional units and studying student work samples to determine better ways to meet the needs of struggling students. Co-teaching was the next natural step for these inclusive teams, as they saw this as a way to become even more involved together with the learning of their shared students. Putting English and social studies content teachers together and having special education supports in many of the single-content or interdisciplinary sections during unit instruction and activities became a very typical class structure. Each interdisciplinary team had to take the next step from just sharing information and doing some planning together, to actually moving into co-teaching instructional practice for portions of each unit. The PLC members already felt rather comfortable in giving and receiving input on student or curricular issues, but now also had to commit to teaching together and sharing both instructional space and time. They had to work through their initial feelings of apprehension at being "watched" by a PLC colleague during joint instruction via critical conversations that focused on individual fears, motives, and then joint goals and objectives for the students and the co-teaching process. Continual time together in co-planning and co-teaching resulted in units totally created, taught, and co-owned by interdisciplinary teaching teams—not just contributed to by PLC members.

It is in these close, collaborative teaching relationships that essential changes can be made as a team within the actual context of real and ongoing teaching practice. Co-teachers can experiment with different teaching methods in real time, and they have a greater ability to quickly and accurately assess student learning and challenges, so that time is not wasted unnecessarily in adjusting or modifying curriculum or interventions.

Response to Intervention

Just as the increased emphasis on assessment and other accurate data on student learning provided by co-teachers enhances schools with PLC cultures, it can also inform the response to intervention framework now cited in the revised Individuals With Disabilities Education Improvement Act of 2004. Previously, practitioners used an IQ-achievement discrepancy formula to determine a student's qualification for learning disabilities (LD), but now, because of the 2004 legislation, the alternative RTI framework can be used (Fuchs & Fuchs, 2006). Because RTI is a schoolwide set of procedures to promote successful academic and behavior outcomes for students, it complements both the PLC concept and co-teaching. Decisions in RTI are based on student data and need, and they occur within a multitier system of curriculum and intervention options (Martínez & Nellis, 2008). Both general and special educators are key decision makers in determining instructional interventions for students, because these professionals are the first line of direct instruction in classrooms. Co-teachers can base these decisions on even more accurate and direct student data culled from interactions with students on a continual basis. Additional insights can be gathered from paraprofessionals, school psychologists, administrators, parents, and other related service personnel—all of whom may have direct contact with co-teachers, but often more indirect service to students.

The student data gathered by co-teachers through RTI then culminate in problem solving and experimentation to determine new or adapted curricula or methods with ongoing assessment and evaluation at predetermined intervals (Murawski & Hughes, 2009). Response to intervention and co-teaching are easily incorporated concurrently, as they have a natural relationship to the real daily practice of teaching in classrooms—and they work together to provide quality instruction for students with adequate professional support for teachers.

Willow Creek Intermediate School: Shawn and Jen

Willow Creek, the intermediate school (grades 4 through 8) in the Allen School Corporation, is in the first year of implementing their own model of response to intervention. It is also the first year for Shawn (a special educator) and Jen (a general educator) to co-teach at the fifth-grade level, focusing most of their work together in language arts and math instruction. In prior years, the two teachers have always planned jointly with minimal actual co-teaching. This year they took a leap into total co-teaching for these two content areas. Although both teachers were initially hesitant to move from their comfort zones into curricular or instructional adaptations within the school's RTI model, Shawn and Jen wanted to attempt a more holistic way of addressing the continuing needs of students in language arts and math. They took small beginning steps by continuing their co-planning in both content areas, but only engaging in co-teaching in math as a starting point. This content seemed easier to start with, since the skills and curriculum were very hierarchically structured, and using their paraeducator as an additional support with student math groupings fit most easily into the schedule. Once they mildly struggled getting comfortable with teaching together in one classroom, they were able to increase the amount of co-teaching time in math; they then slowly added co-teaching in the language arts curriculum to the co-planning they were already doing in that content. Using units as their structural boundaries, Shawn and Jen were able to try more varieties of ways to assess and group students, and co-teach in creative ways.

By using a comprehensive data collection and analysis process, they could easily see that these content areas of language arts and math were the academic areas where more special education students required assistance to fully engage in the general education curriculum. These were the same content areas that lent themselves well to assessment, planned intervention groups, and progress monitoring of all students that needed to occur so that students would get the most advantage out of the school's RTI model.

Shawn and Jen are now collaborating on the curriculum-based assessments and grouping and regrouping decisions as to how to work with students at varying levels in language arts and math. Their constant conversations focusing on assessment, placement, specific intervention, and time-limited results keep them on top of all student performance in an ongoing fashion. The teachers also utilize additional input from the paraeducator assigned to students they share, having her gather assessment data and support one of the instructional groups in math. Shawn and Jen look at all of this information on a weekly basis to make decisions to adjust group membership, adapt or modify curricula content to match various student needs, and constantly monitor student performance. The implementation of daily co-teaching practice for these fifth-grade teachers has meshed quickly and effectively with their RTI practices.

Differentiated Instruction

Quality instruction is a cornerstone of the teaching and learning process. One of the best practices within the research literature for meeting the needs of a diverse student body in schools today is differentiated instruction. With DI, teachers can utilize a framework that recognizes and accounts for learner variance within instructional planning (Tomlinson & McTighe, 2006). In DI, when planning lessons and units of instruction, teachers must consider the content, process, and products and differentiate in ways that are meaningful to students but do not compromise the quality of material coverage. Having co-teachers work in concert to assess, brainstorm, plan, create, and evaluate these considerations for students is an asset to the total teaching process.

Two teachers bring different sets of knowledge about their students and academic content to their classroom. They use this diverse knowledge to guide them in planning ways to differentiate based on students' variances in learning—their learner profiles, learner readiness, or learner interests (Tomlinson, 2001). Combining their assets, the goal of co-teachers in DI is to decide what has to be taught (required by state standards) by considering what they want students to know, understand, and be able to do (Tomlinson & McTighe, 2006).

Blomquist High School: Lara and June

Lara and June have been co-teaching for two years in a high school math class at Blomquist High School. These two teachers are experienced in using differentiated instruction as a natural part of both their individual and joint teaching styles. Both the special and general educator in this partnership tend to think of their content as a menu of strategies to teach while providing students with different ways to demonstrate their learning. Lara and June have worked with DI so long as separate teachers, that in moving to a co-taught arrangement, neither could conceptualize a better way to reach the diversity of students in their math class. Both teachers were able to think creatively about all of the possible options they could make available to students to help in differentiating the math content for students' varied learning profiles, readiness, and interests. The tougher part was figuring out how they could prioritize and make final decisions on the best ways to use DI within each lesson or unit without overwhelming themselves in the planning or their students in the instruction. After some trial and error of taking on too much, or not giving students explicit enough instructions, Lara and June were able to move forward in their joint work in a fully differentiated, co-taught math class. Brainstorming ideas for content, process, and product, making quality decisions on best options for each student group, and then sharing the teaching has become a way of life in Lara and June's class.

Universal Design for Learning

A final related and relevant area within the context of school reform and the rationale for co-teaching is that of universal design for learning. This is not a single model, but rather a set of principles for curriculum development that focuses on improving student learning. UDL is also well matched with the reform of school learning environments and methods. Having its genesis in the universal accessibility of physical structures, UDL has evolved to ensure that students with and without disabilities have access to multiple means of representation, multiple means of action and expression, and multiple means of engagement (Rose & Meyer, 2002).

Universal design for learning recognizes the three brain networks that are involved in any learning: the recognition networks, the "what" of learning; the strategic networks, the "how" of learning; and the affective networks, the "why" of learning. Again, each co-teacher can utilize his or her distinct knowledge of students to create and implement lessons so that student variances in recognition learning, strategic learning, and affective learning are supported appropriately. Brainstorming, planning, creating, and implementing in the teaching and learning process are magnified by the power of two when co-teachers work together for the benefit of all students. Co-teachers who recognize the power of UDL as a daily application in diverse classrooms have the potential to increase student achievement and their own professional development within their joint classroom contexts.

A PATINS Project: Northern Indiana High School Teachers

Since 2003, the PATINS Project (Promoting Achievement Through Technology and Instruction for All Students), has supported schools throughout Indiana in implementing UDL principles, especially in literacy and math (Hershman, n.d.). Across the United States, there are other state programs also focused on assistive technology systems–change initiatives. Teachers in elementary, middle, and high schools have written grant proposals and been accepted into the UDL support programs by PATINS, in addition to having their lesson and unit plans as a part of the state website. Each school-based project supported by a PATINS grant must show how the lessons or units utilize multiple means of representation, action and expression, and engagement in creating learning opportunities for diverse student populations. A small group of northern Indiana high school teachers (general, special, and technology education) who also engage in co-teaching in American history courses collaboratively developed five UDL units that engage students' varying abilities in the state standards and content of American history. Their co-teaching work helped during the planning process to determine what all students, most students, and some students would know by the end of each unit. The co-teachers took what had been typical American history content and infused the units with technology that enhanced each student's ability for various aspects of recognition learning, strategic learning, and affective learning. Getting two or three teachers to agree on the key elements of each lesson and then the crucial ways in which technology might support students with their learning was a challenge. Negotiations, along with some heated discussions, preceded the beginnings of their work together, but they continued to remind each other of the ultimate goal of their work: increased learning and engagement for all students, especially those who had typically been reluctant learners in previous history courses.

These UDL units were instrumental in creating engaging learning environments for all students, supported by improved technology and co-teaching methods that were the impetus for moving forward in new teaching and learning directions. With the lesson content developed by a team of professionals, teaching pairs or teams helped implement these quality units for all American history students in the high school. Universal design for learning was a natural outgrowth of the planning team's creative work with their diverse groups of students.

Outcomes

As you read and work through the questions, activities, and examples in the critical conversations in co-teaching that follow, we invite you to engage in a very active way with us. The following priority outcomes are yours if you are fully engaged in the text. You will:

- Realize there is research literature and a theoretical basis for quality practice in teaching in general, and co-teaching specifically

- Understand the importance of adding value on a daily basis in your own classrooms by actively putting the co-teaching concepts to use

- Utilize the various reflective questions, conversations, models, tools, examples, and scenarios here using the critical conversations framework

- Find your own best professional practices and the specific ways in which you add value to the classroom with a co-teaching partner as you work together to design, plan, implement, assess, and evaluate your work

- Engage in professional development within your classroom and school as you co-teach

- Understand the benefits of the value-added collaborative framework to improve professional practices through co-teaching

- Know how to assess your co-teaching partnership on a developmental continuum

- Know how to access additional valuable skills, tools, and resources designed to engage professional colleagues in meaningful dialogue and lead to value-added shared practice

Now that you have finished the opening invitation into co-teaching conversations, we invite you to venture deeper with us in exploring, experimenting, conversing, problem solving, and taking your co-teaching further in daily practice. We believe the journey is a worthwhile one that will benefit co-teaching partners, their students, and their school communities.

2

CO-TEACHING MODELS

Conversation Starters

- What ways of teaching and support are available to help us increase our support for students?
- What co-teaching models can we use in our collaborative practice?
- What can we learn from the stories of other co-teachers?
- What are the lessons learned from teachers who have used these co-teaching strategies?

Support for students can take many forms along the continuum of ways of teaching. Co-teaching is an effective, evidence-based option. Other strategies include consultation, collaborative teaming, and services offered by instructional aides. In this chapter, we briefly discuss each of these options. Then we describe three sets of co-teaching strategies for you to consider, illustrated by stories from teachers who are successfully implementing them in elementary, middle, and high school classrooms. We conclude the chapter with a list of the overall benefits, challenges, and lessons learned using these co-teaching models to enhance your professional practice.

A Continuum of Support for Students

First, we offer a definition of collaboration. *Collaboration* is an interactive process in which colleagues share ideas, strategies, and tools in teams, committees, and departments within schools. Effective collaborative interactions can lead to shared decision making and shared teaching to attain instructional goals that improve learning for all students. Collaboration is an essential ingredient in each of these strategies. It is crucial if you hope to be effective as a co-teaching partner.

Consultation

In the consultation model, educators receive support from a consultant who provides expertise, technical assistance, and resources. Generally consultants do not share in the delivery of instruction. *Internal consultants* are colleagues who come from within your school or district, such as a speech and language expert who provides help to a general educator on how to embed strategies to help particular students in need of language interventions. *External consultants* might be private consultants, vendors, university personnel, or other experts. An example of an external consultant is a specialist who provides consultation and technical assistance through professional development workshops and ongoing embedded coaching and support as teachers begin to implement new methods of instruction or practice. Typical examples in schools might include positive behavior support specialists, differentiated instruction coordinators, and literacy coaches.

Collaborative Teaming

Collaborative teams participate in interactive processes in which members share ideas, strategies, and tools in their schools. Here too effective collaborative interactions can lead to shared decision making and attainment of shared goals that are designed to improve learning for all students. Teams take many forms, such as grade-level or content teams, core teams, academic teams, curricular-mapping teams, textbook adoption teams, response to intervention teams, IEP conferencing teams, and creative problem-solving teams such as instructional consultation teams. Some teams are long-standing and share in the delivery of instruction, while others are convened to make informed decisions that support instruction and address a particular student need. All of these teams help bring a more holistic approach to creative problem solving by adding collective wisdom and additional expertise to improve planning and implementation of quality instruction.

Supportive Instructional Aides

Supportive instructional teaching assistants and paraprofessionals, the third model of the service delivery system, often play vital roles by providing adapted or modified instruction to support students who may have specific difficulties in mastering material or who exhibit behavior issues. In some instances, these supports are limited to one-on-one assistance. Sometimes the supports offer no more than crowd control. Occasionally, well-trained and motivated support personnel are able to contribute high-level skill and expertise, closer to the role of a co-teaching partnership. However, be cautious when incorporating supportive instructional assistants because they are generally not licensed professional educators and therefore are limited in their ability to provide planning and other services on their own. Licensing and regulations must be carefully followed.

Co-Teaching

Co-teaching is an effective, evidence-based instructional strategy in which two or more caring professionals share responsibility for a group of students and work collaboratively to add instructional value to enhance their efforts. The partners contribute their expertise in content and instructional strategies to improve student learning. When executed well and supported sufficiently, co-teaching is one of the most effective instructional strategies teachers can use. In an effective partnership, co-teaching can provide rigorous professional development opportunities for teachers when it is ongoing and embedded.

It is important to remember that co-teaching is neither a comprehensive school improvement model nor a situation in which one teacher (usually the general educator) teaches and the other (usually the special educator) drifts around the classroom, or in which the special educator only works with his or her students while other students in the class struggle to learn.

Typically, we think of co-teaching partnerships that are made up of a special educator and a general educator, but numerous combinations are being used in an attempt to address a growing diversity of student needs. Possibilities abound when we share responsibility for our students by collaborating to make better instructional matches and enhance instructional strategies. Creative colleagues often look for nontraditional co-teaching partners, such as English learning specialists, occupational therapists, physical therapists, speech language pathologists, fine arts faculty, technology instructors, Title I literacy teachers, and guidance counselors. If they are willing and schedules permit, these specialists can be some of the most exciting and rewarding partners because they are seldom asked or included in regular teaching assignments. Many of them relish the opportunity to use their knowledge and skills in more creative and meaningful ways with students and colleagues.

Co-Teaching as a Model to Achieve Outcomes

When we first began our work, our professional development focused on promoting traditional co-teaching models. While this approach has effectively helped hundreds of teaching pairs, we started to observe some interesting things. Far too many teachers were more focused on the how-tos of model application at the expense of building relationships with their partners. Other teachers were fixated on naming particular models and attempting to replicate a rigid prescription. No textbook, video clip, or workshop alone can provide you with the skills, knowledge, *and* the application of co-teaching strategies in your classrooms. All too often teachers were getting discouraged and losing heart because they weren't following prescribed models exactly. Even with our encouragement, some teachers were hesitant to adopt and modify the models to meet their own styles and contexts.

It soon became clear to us that if we helped partners focus their efforts on their relationships and on student outcomes, they would be more effective in their instructional design planning and implementation. As teachers, we want to successfully match students' prior knowledge and experiences with what the curriculum standards dictate. And yet we all struggle to help students who exhibit an increasingly wider variety of learning needs and abilities, expectations, preferences, interests, and motivations for learning. We have found that when intentional conversations among teachers guide important decisions about instruction, teachers choose more appropriate student groupings and design and implement more authentic instruction. This process has proven much more productive than focusing on traditional co-teaching models alone.

Because time is limited and demands continue to grow, we have modified and streamlined more traditional co-teaching models into three categories. The least intense are the complementary models in which one teacher takes the lead and the other teacher adds value in a variety of supportive ways. The second group, side-by-side co-teaching, offers opportunities for both teachers to be more actively engaged in the teaching process by using various student groupings. In the third group, "walking the talk," traditionally known as teaming, each of the adults is actively involved in all aspects of the instructional design and implementation of instruction.

Following a brief description of each of the three categories, we provide scenarios from a variety of classrooms illustrating how teachers are successfully implementing these co-teaching strategies.

Complementary Co-Teaching

In complementary co-teaching models, both teachers set learning goals about the content of the unit or lesson and plan how instruction will be delivered. A lead teacher provides specific instruction for the entire class while the second teacher provides *intentional* observations or *targeted* support by performing tasks such as helping students stay on task, modeling note taking, or demonstrating a desired behavior for individual students or groups. The second teacher could also make *intentional* observations of student or teacher behaviors for the partners to use to inform future strategies and support.

The Benefits of Complementary Co-Teaching

Complementary variations of co-teaching are a great place for partners to begin. Especially if intentional, selective, and used sparingly, this strategy gives you and your partner a way to launch your shared practice. Experienced co-teachers can use complementary strategies to increase engagement and inform subsequent interventions. For many co-teachers, this may be one of the first entries into quality professional dialogue they have experienced. Students report that the personalized and specific attention they receive helps them establish better relationships with adults. The model "buys time" for the partnership to develop; the general educator may feel a loss of integrity in the content unless he or she is able to take the lead in instruction. On the other hand, special educators can be eased out of their comfort zone and into general education content and an inclusive setting by gradually engaging in instruction.

Both special and general educators may encounter differing core beliefs about their students for the first time. More often than not, special educators are pleasantly surprised to find that students with identified needs are happier and are also performing to the higher standards that may be present in the general education classes. General education students have an opportunity to increase their understanding and empathy for diverse students.

The Challenges of Complementary Co-Teaching

Too much of a good thing is not good. As helpful and supportive as observations and minimal direct student or teacher support can be, teachers can easily get stuck using this least-intensive model as their default mode. When they fall victim to keeping the same roles as supporter or observer and lead teacher, they give subtle but powerful messages to students about who is in charge and who helps. Unless teachers interchange roles occasionally, a few phenomena happen: students do not see the partners as equal, students may feel they are being stigmatized because they are targets of extra attention and support, and one teacher comes to "own" the content expertise while the other co-teacher might be able to hide behind IEP goals as a way to stay with his or her identified students.

When co-teachers fail to plan together, it becomes easy for the lead teacher to make all of the instructional decisions, leaving the special educator in a role more akin to an instructional aide. In fact, it is not uncommon to find support teachers in the classroom who are hard pressed to name either the learning goals for the class on a particular day or a way that they have added value in the classroom.

Another challenge some complementary co-teachers face is what to do with observation data. Observation data are of little value if you don't share them with your partner and discuss how the information can be used to enhance your teaching, increase student engagement, address behavior issues, or inform other pertinent outcomes.

Complementary Co-Teaching in Practice

The following co-teaching stories show complementary co-teaching in practice, illustrating the value of observation and the value of providing minimal direct support for students. This model also offers a good starting point that allows new partnerships to develop trust in one another. The first story comes from a school district that is enmeshed in a professional learning community (PLC) initiative. We focus on a first-grade interdisciplinary team using complementary co-teaching variations to enhance instruction for their English learners. The second story describes an eager middle school math teacher who uses a number of complementary co-teaching models to increase the engagement not only of his students but also of his reluctant special education partner.

Elementary Complementary Co-Teaching: One Teach, One Observe and Support

Fred and Sam often merge their separate classes of first graders in a large conference room to co-teach lessons or units they have planned together. At midterm, they also invited Sue, the speech pathologist, to observe her first-grade English learners during these joint efforts. The three had been sharing evidence-based practices and had problem solved on a daily basis for the past year. Unlike many of the teachers in her school, Sue felt that these two colleagues actually saw her as a valuable resource—so much so that over lunch one day, Fred and Sam challenged her to "get with the program" and start co-teaching with them. At first she took it as their way to humor her, but when she heard about their vision and expectations for all of the first graders, she discovered common ground.

Instead of continuing to pull several of her students from their first-grade classrooms daily for therapy sessions in her room, the trio came up with strategies to do that work in the classrooms. In the early stages of the co-teaching partnership, Sue offered valuable observation and support in a variety of ways. For instance, Fred led an interactive lesson using a whiteboard to check for understanding of letter sounds and basic word vocabulary while Sam recorded individual responses that targeted students made on their individual whiteboards. As Fred and Sam taught either the whole class or various groupings, Sue was able to observe the EL students, listening for how they were able to apply the skills she was working on in their speech language sessions. She soon supplemented her observations by providing additional support to her students in the general education setting as her colleagues continued their lessons. To the trio's delight, many of her strategies have benefited other students as well as her EL students.

This story is a great example of how often beginning teams start with a small repertoire of complementary practices and quickly build to more complex models. Sue was convinced that analyzing her observation data with such caring and effective teachers helped her students benefit from more authentic uses for their language skills both in the classroom and in their lives. She was able to increase the students' motivation to perform for her and also make more authentic connections between what was happening in the general education classes and speech and language sessions. In addition, her partners gave her a better understanding of the process of providing age- and context-appropriate quality instructional design and instruction for larger groups.

Sam and Fred reported that before collaborating with Sue, they really didn't have a clear enough idea what their speech students were doing when they were pulled out for services. As they analyzed the observation data, all three of these teachers were able to work on similar vocabulary and comprehension skills. Sue was able to contribute in planning sessions eventually embedding the unit designs into her own sessions, giving her a connection to the learning outcomes for the first time in her years of working in the school. English learners and other struggling students were not singled out, but rather benefited from more modeling from peers. Sam and Fred felt they were able to support Sue's efforts, integrating new skills and opportunities for the students to practice their new language skills throughout the day. All three professionals would say they feel the other students in the class also share the commitment to be more inclusive and intentional in their support of their EL classmates.

Secondary Complementary Co-Teaching: One Teach, One Observe and Support

Claudia had just gotten used to providing meaningful observations, debriefing with her partner and occasionally directly offering minimal support. She could not imagine doing more. She felt major trepidation when asked to move her students from a self-contained resource room into general education core subject classrooms. Her new assignment meant that she would be co-teaching with Joe, a beloved math teacher. She was also carrying around some pretty big fears: (1) she had devised her own math curriculum in the resource room and was terrified she might not be able to master the math program recently adopted, (2) she predicted that general education would be the ruination of her "helpless" students, and (3) she had already checked, and she didn't have enough money to retire. Resigned to give it a try, she figured she could at least observe and support her students. Claudia might even find some creativity to add value by observing and offering minimal support for Joe's instruction. The modus operandi for the pre-algebra class they shared twice a day began with Joe presenting new material to the whole group while the students took notes and solved problems in small collaborative groups.

Claudia and Joe came up with a variety of complementary co-teaching activities. They felt the students directly benefited in several of the supporting activities Claudia performed for individuals and small groups. In addition, her observations informed their practice by providing them with insights Joe would not have discovered without her. The following list provides a sampling of the results the team attributed to their beginning co-teaching classes wherein Joe handled direct instruction and Claudia collected observation data or performed minor support roles for students and for Joe.

What Claudia did while Joe instructed:

- Collected observation data
- Supported individual students, small groups of students, and Joe
- Supported with her modifications and adjusted assignments according to IEPs
- Pretaught and retaught new content to struggling students

What they learned about this strategy:

- Claudia and Joe conducted more meaningful preassessments.
- Students were more engaged with the curriculum.
- Co-teaching increased students' interaction with the adults.
- They offered increased proximity and added wait time.
- They were able to ultimately increase actual instructional time because of more appropriate student groupings.
- Students realized benefits through the preteaching and reteaching of necessary academic skills, clarification of behavioral expectations, and improved instructional matches based on student mistakes.

- Claudia's math confidence level and feeling that she was contributing to the class goals increased.

After the partners had mastered the complementary strategies, they became aware of the importance of having their math students incorporate 21st century skills of critical thinking, decision making, problem solving, and so on into their daily lives. Claudia and Joe's support became more intentional as they embedded those skills into their lessons. The same principle applied to Bloom's taxonomy; Joe had always wanted to be more intentional with the taxonomy, knowing it would help increase the students' higher-order thinking skills, especially in mathematical problem solving. Again, Claudia's observations served as a preassessment to determine how they would incorporate strategies to highlight those principles into their presentations and assignments. Using these complementary roles helped them model and observe the kinds of responses they hoped to elicit from their students. Together they developed a short checklist to help with their observations so they could more easily determine exactly where the students were having difficulty with follow through.

While Joe focused on the content reviews and tests, Claudia was able to help to rectify mistakes due to confusion in testing organization and timing by giving appropriate prompts and cues to assist them. Supporting all of the students in the room soon had an added advantage over Claudia taking students to the resource room. Before the partnership, she would typically pull students out for remediation, causing them to miss key connections to prior learning as well as losing access to critical pieces of the general curriculum that were being presented during the pull-out time. Using the complementary variations, Joe remained confident that all of the students were being given more authentic testing situations.

At first the pair benefited from the specific data Claudia collected, using them to help make better decisions about how students were grouped and given supports. Because Joe had worried about Claudia's unfamiliarity with his content, he was able to more clearly state the learning goals for her and the students. A process slowly emerged that demonstrated the commitment both teachers had for student learning and played to the strengths of each teacher. Claudia became more comfortable with the content, so both teachers were seen as math teachers able to support all of the students. Joe began to see that the observations they debriefed increased their repertoire of strategies and adaptations not just for the identified students, but for the whole class. Ever respectful of her comfort level, but still wanting to stretch her expertise, there were times Joe switched roles with Claudia during their second period if he felt she would be able to take the lead. Feeling she still had lowered expectations for her identified students, Joe came up with a plan to raise her expectations of the students and stop the practice of automatically taking the identified students to the resource room to read their tests to them. These complementary strategies allowed the teachers to design a number of universal supports after paying attention to the barriers they were experiencing in the learning process. As Joe and Claudia provided more supports, the students began asking to stay in their classroom during testing situations, and soon the lines began to blur concerning which students "belonged" to Joe and which to Claudia. Both teachers were also much more helpful in providing the kinds of supports the students really benefited from as opposed to the old strategies of giving everyone extra time, calculators, or lowered expectations.

Joe has been more than happy to maintain control over the content, but he has already begun to think about ways to increase Claudia's contributions, confident that she will quickly get up to speed with her math expertise. They have both become enthusiastic about the possibility of an increase in the percentage of students passing pre-algebra because of the increased personal attention they are able to give students now that they are working well in groups.

Unless Joe had stretched Claudia's contributions, she might still be offering minimal efforts and feeling like an underutilized professional, and their principal would be questioning whether he was getting sufficient return on his investment. In the end, the complementary model bought them some time to develop a partnership that now is able to move easily between those early strategies and side-by-side and teaming strategies as well. The decisions are now based on the instructional needs of the students, not the comfort level or expectations of adults.

We have offered several ways that complementary co-teaching can add value to instruction. Many beginning teams start with a small repertoire of complementary practices and quickly build to more complex models. The next set of models allows more equal participation and direct instruction by each adult in the partnership.

Side-by-Side Co-Teaching

Each of the side-by-side partners contributes more intensely to decisions about curriculum and instruction for their students. The difference in this strategy is in how the class is divided for actual instruction: in a large- and small-group configuration, in halves, or in stations or learning centers. Co-teachers alternate roles and responsibilities, so each teacher is able to work with students in both a primary and a supportive role. We discuss three kinds of side-by-side strategies; they are dependent on the arrangement of the environment and the purposeful groupings of students:

1 A typical side-by-side alternative strategy involves one educator instructing a larger group and the other teacher taking responsibility for a smaller alternative group. Frequently co-teachers begin by using preteaching, reteaching, or offering enrichment activities for these alternative groupings, but there are so many other effective uses when both teachers share responsibility for planning and instruction. Groupings may center on readiness levels, learning styles, student interests, or particular tasks assigned.

2 Sometimes co-teachers use a side-by-side strategy by dividing the class into fairly even groups. Each of the teachers focuses his or her instruction on the same content or closely related, but they vary their delivery styles or differentiate content or process. They may choose to bring the larger group back together at key points or keep the groups separate throughout the class period. Both teachers share responsibility for planning and instruction. An effective use of this strategy is for the teachers to agree on power standards they will focus on for a particular lesson and then divide the group into smaller sections. One group will be expected to meet the minimum standard, while the other group will use the basic power standard as their starting point and extend their learning from there. Another variation would be to take an issue or unit of content and have each group present differing views. Students in each group learn one particular issue or portion of the unit in depth, and then both groups share their content, expanding their breadth of understanding by hearing from the other group and expanding their depth of understanding by having an opportunity to teach their own content.

3 The final strategy is to set up side-by-side learning centers or stations with students and teachers divided into a variety of teacher-led groupings and independent study opportunities. Learning centers or stations require even more intense planning and collaboration than the other side-by-side strategies. Two or more educators can be quite creative in how

they share all space, time, and instructional processes with their students. Rather than sharing the same duties or splitting the students into two groups, the co-teachers offer students a wider variety of options. Students may rotate through stations on a predetermined schedule while teachers repeat instructions to each group that comes through. Additional stations may be used for students to complete work assignments; to participate in peer tutoring; to have appropriate behaviors modeled; or to work under the supervision of a student teacher, paraeducator, or other adult available in the classroom. Stations can also be designed to operate independent of teachers, with students following instructions at technology work stations. Delivery may vary according to student needs as long as the teachers have agreed on the curriculum to be presented.

The Benefits of Side-by-Side Co-Teaching

This model provides an excellent vehicle to give students full access to the general education curriculum and still differentiate by dividing students on the basis of their interests, abilities, and learning preferences. Students report they receive more intensive interaction in smaller, more focused groupings with more adults who want to help them learn. In addition, this strategy provides an excellent opportunity in which to use other educators and specialists, as well as community volunteer experts as station facilitators.

The Challenges of Side-by-Side Co-Teaching

Side-by-side co-teaching requires planning, timing presentations, and matching pacing. Co-teachers must watch for messages that might perpetuate a sense that some students are in a self-contained class in the middle of a general education setting. It is also possible that struggling students may become stigmatized if they are kept in the small groups receiving all of the interventions. These strategies all contain elements that could easily cause some students to feel overwhelmed or confused, such as movement between groupings and activities, transition times, noise levels, and changing pace. The teaching partners must be mindful of the time and activities students could miss when grouped for other activities.

Some co-teaching partners could also be resistant to trying these particular strategies for the same reasons. Teachers would be remiss, however, if they didn't differentiate purpose and activities so that multiple groupings and models of co-teaching can be implemented. Valuable instructional time could be saved by being proactive and spending time front-loading by teaching protocols for moving students around and determining processes for selecting student groupings for stations.

Side-by-Side Models in Practice

The variations we present to illustrate side-by-side teaching are dependent on student needs, partner trust, planning time, curricular expertise, and grouping options. You will read about a first-grade class where the teachers group students for phonemic awareness and a second-grade co-teaching pair that facilitates stations during a vocabulary-recognition lesson. A middle school language arts partnership example shows how they are able to provide their students with deeper levels of reflection and higher order thinking skills. The high school examples concluding this section show how language arts and science classes can benefit by teachers using co-teachers as side-by-side models.

Elementary Side-by-Side Co-Teaching: Parallel

First-grade teachers Cal and Zak, and Velma, the paraprofessional who had been helping support students in the building for close to six years, make up an informal, albeit very collaborative team. That is to say, they have not been assigned to co-teach by their principal; they just believe it makes good pedagogical sense. The three adults work together to help the first graders learn to identify initial, medial, and final sounds in one-syllable words. They began this effort by dividing the group. Cal, Zak, and Velma each take one third of the students to focus on a particular position of the sound in words: Cal's group identifies medial sounds, Zak's group identifies final sounds, and Velma's group identifies initial sounds. In each of the groups, the students are asked to play a game identifying the sound and its position. They repeat this lesson for three days for each sound.

The students are arranged into small clusters based on preassessments administered the first week of school. One of the three teachers visits each of the small groups to reteach, review, and preteach struggling students with key concepts of phonemic awareness, tapping into their learning styles. Velma teaches phonemic awareness to a small group using a variety of skill-development activities the students need. Olivia, the Title I teacher, will occasionally work with the cluster of EL students and students with limited prior knowledge. Flexible groupings are common throughout the day in this classroom.

Because they share a large room, the teachers feel that the multiple groupings allow them to target the important early language arts skills in a much more focused way, adding more engagement for students, and differentiating according to several different emphases—for example, interests, abilities, aptitudes, reading level, and multiple intelligences. Cal and Zak are quick to credit their principal for supporting their instructional decisions and giving them the flexibility to call others in when needed, and merge their classes, and they gladly provide evidence of their efforts as a way to ensure accountability and continue their work together.

Elementary Side-by-Side Co-Teaching: Learning Centers or Stations

Caryn and Matt share a second-grade classroom down the hall from Cal and Zak. They often joke that their shared practice may seem more like creative chaos, but it is working, according to the high achievement of their students on yearly examinations. Caryn and Matt have their vocabulary recognition stations down to a system. They became believers in using assessment data to find instructional matches for their vastly diverse students. Having seen the power of keeping students engaged and making instructional matches throughout the day, they decided to spend sufficient time the first few weeks of the school year teaching station etiquette with clear expectations, timing, and transition protocols. They have dedicated four locations in the room for permanent stations and have prepared materials so that with very little effort, they can use all four for language arts in the morning and math or science in the afternoon.

An example of language arts stations might include the following: station one—vocabulary skill building; station two—word definitions and context clues; station three—independent computer game; and station four—independent, interactive whiteboard activity that connects new vocabulary words with other fifth-grade subject areas.

Through varying the thematic focus frequently, Caryn and Matt are able to extend the results to a wider range of their curriculum. They are also able to design each station to include assessments that will help them understand their students' skills better, and track their progress quickly as they move through the stations and weeks of the curriculum. These co-teachers believe that their complex and occasionally chaotic work together using quality, preplanned station assessments and activities has helped them verify that no part of the curriculum is haphazard, and for every student there is a plan of growth and development.

Elementary Side-by-Side Co-Teaching: Parallel, Regroupings

For two days, Eve read a short biography of a historical figure aloud to one half of her eighth-grade language arts class and asked the students to identify main characters. Hank did the same thing with the other half of the class using a different biography. Then the students were divided into three different groups and asked to discuss different aspects of each of the story's subjects. Eve facilitated the group focused on physical traits, Hank led the group focused on personality traits, and a third group was given a list of websites to check out to find additional factors to inform a discussion about personalities. Each group was to record the major points of their conversations and findings. The third day, the whole class met with both Eve and Hank to share their findings in a jigsaw format. From that discussion, they were to compare and contrast various aspects from the biographies, and also discuss how each of the characters in their stories changed and grew.

Eve and Hank incorporated another strategy into their class. They decided that stations could be especially effective to help the students delve into longer reading selections when studying literature. Because many of their students struggle with vocabulary and have reading levels far below most of the print material available to them, the teachers used a lot of visuals, including movies, to introduce or explore literary selections. They set up a number of independent and group stations to teach the class how to use relevant tools and resources to help with their comprehension. Station activities included a worksheet to compare and contrast a movie clip and a book section, a Venn diagram of different character traits, cartoon drawings, dramatizations, written analysis of characterization, and graphic organizers to make timelines of plot.

Because Eve and Hank are already sold on using stations as a way to ensure instructional matches, they are willing to put in the time and have become very effective and efficient in their designs. The students always find a wide variety of ways to make connections and be successful in this rich learning environment.

These teachers were interested in increasing comprehension and also getting deeper levels of reflection and higher-order thinking with their students. By using smaller groups and more targeted focuses for each, the students were able to go deeper and broader, which was reflected in the classroom discussions.

Middle School Side-by-Side Co-Teaching: Parallel Regroupings

Having taught in a neighboring district for a dozen years, Marta is in her first year teaching an intermediate multiage class (grades 4 and 5) at the new Promising Practices School. Her new school has only been open a few months. The school had actively recruited her for her expertise and previous successes facilitating writers' workshops.

Charlie was to have been chairman of the English department at the local community college next year. Unfortunately, the announcement of his chair came at about the same time as his pink slip notifying him that he would not have a teaching position for the coming year due to budget issues. When he went to Promising Practices to register his own children, the administrator convinced him to apply, touting their school's strong community support, shared vision, and the lively and creative faculty she had assembled. Charlie jumped at the chance, thankful to have any teaching position given the economic situation in the community. But shortly after he accepted, he began to have misgivings. He learned that all of the classes in this new school were taught collaboratively. How had he missed this in the interview? He knew he was a really good high school teacher, perhaps a great teacher of older students. He certainly didn't need a co-teacher because of his own inadequacies, even though he did wonder about transferring his skills to an intermediate classroom. And he couldn't imagine working closely with someone else, especially given his content expertise and experience. From the start, he respected his co-teacher Marta, and yet he remained unconvinced he was cut out for collaborative practices. He certainly didn't feel positive about her writers' workshop approach. In fact, he had never used this technique in all of his teaching. Both teachers began the year with lots of trepidation.

Together they agreed that Marta would introduce the first of many planned writers' workshops to the whole group. Typically, she would teach a minilesson to explain and demonstrate the content, tools, and materials the students would use during their workshop. Charlie would assist all of the students, alternating among small groups of students organized into writing clubs that he and Marta had preassigned. The groupings were based on their preassessment student inventories, the kinds of writing students liked to read, and how well they worked in cooperative groupings.

Charlie quickly saw that by using writing clubs, students had access to differentiated choices, enabling him to provide much more meaningful feedback and support than he had imagined using traditional means. Both teachers quickly came to appreciate one another's contributions to the content and the support they offered during the workshops. An unintended consequence of their partnership was Charlie's realization that rather than having his gifts and talents underutilized at this intermediate level, his eager and responsive audience awaited his gift of teaching, thereby renewing his love of teaching writing. The fact that he could help shape this critical content with young students and impact their learning goals so positively made him feel proud.

Marta was able to continue teaching her passion for the writers' workshop approach, but by collaborating with Charlie, she is better able to meet all of the diverse needs of their students. She admitted that in the past she tended to only see benefits of the writers' workshop approach, mainly for the high achievers. Charlie has brought a solid foundation and a higher academic level. They both feel they can incorporate new strategies and resources they are learning from each other. Together, Marta and Charlie have helped their students exceed their state standardized test scores in writing. They plan to experiment with this workshop approach to increase student engagement by trying it in other subject areas. They feel they can help their students achieve much deeper levels of meaning with their combined knowledge and support.

High School Side-by-Side Co-Teaching: Alternative

English teachers Cassie and Max and the special educator, Rebecca, combine their expertise to implement a unit to support students' understanding, interpreting, analyzing, and synthesizing of a literary work. They provide support interchangeably and use a coaching approach they picked up from a writing initiative in the district earlier in the year. They generally begin with heterogeneous groups and then move to a variation of the alternative model as they introduce a new literary work to three preselected groups according to varying ability levels or by grouping according to specific tasks. All three teachers can facilitate a group. They have modeled and practiced with the students to work in cooperative groupings, so each student assumes a role in the group: for example, facilitator, recorder, referee, time keeper, researcher, or docent. Students occasionally have the choice to work with partners as opposed to the collaborative groups. The tasks vary but always include a demonstration to the larger group showing their group's understanding of a literary concept or an interpretation of an author's writing. The assessments for projects such as this might include a public presentation, product, or demonstration.

Because the students responded so well to this environment and format, the team was able to substitute other literary units using this basic structure. Students in this English class adhere to rigorous standards and at the same time practice their people skills by working together with other students to achieve a common goal, to meet deadlines, and to experience different roles and responsibilities with their peers.

Ruby is in her second year sharing her instructional strategy expertise from special education to general educators at the local high school. Last year she was paired with four different core content teachers, but her principal listened to her well-presented request to narrow her number of content classes she was assigned. She designed her new plan as an attempt to address specific student needs based on their high school's most recent state test score results. The new plan calls for her to specialize by supporting two freshman biology classes with Al and two classes of junior Earth science with Oscar. She incorporates side-by-side models in the biology classes and a variety of complementary and side-by-side models in earth science.

Oscar works with a group of higher achievers to give them some enriched lab time, while Ruby helps the other students prepare for meeting standards in their lab work. All of the students will be assigned to write reviews (similar to the reviews they might find on iTunes or YouTube) to reflect their understanding of the material covered in their respective groups.

Planning for Earth science class is much more extensive, and she and her partner always depend on using preassessments before designing instructional plans. Before presenting each unit, the pair uses an alternative grouping segment to preteach, reteach, or provide enrichment to address the findings of their preassessments. Since all of the students are in multiple groupings on a regular basis, stigmas or issues identifying students' learning needs are never an issue.

Again, as a result of their preassessment of this unit, they were able to easily identify the students who would need some additional help. They use this small-group structure frequently to help students who struggle with science concepts and new vocabulary.

"Walking the Talk" Co-Teaching

"Walking the talk," also known as teaming, happens when two or more teachers share all responsibilities for planning and teaching. Their roles and responsibilities become interchangeable, and the learning activities tend to be more creative and comprehensive. The partners assess and evaluate students, plan and introduce new content, develop skills, clarify information, facilitate learning, handle classroom management, and share instruction for all students, whether that instruction is to an individual, a whole class, or to smaller groups. The adults serve as facilitators, as opposed to delivering traditional lecture and textbook-based lessons. Walking the talk calls for highly competent educators who use whole- and small-group instruction, facilitated and independent stations, observation, and differentiated support in a highly engaging educational environment. As teachers become more comfortable and trusting in their roles as team teachers, they will exhibit more flexibility in lesson presentation. When they have developed the necessary trust, competence, and commitment, students are more engaged because of the additional options they have to learn and demonstrate their progress. Teachers often report that they experience synergy or flow. The adults are continually learning along with the students and are adjusting to the changing needs of their classrooms. Most importantly, students are engaged.

Conventional wisdom suggests that educators are not successful at co-teaching until they are teaming all of the time. While striving to achieve this kind of synergistic approach may be desirable, all of the models presented in this chapter are useful, depending on the learning outcomes you desire. Successful pairs move in and out of all co-teaching models from time to time depending on students, their partnership characteristics, and specific learning goals.

The Benefits of Walking the Talk Co-Teaching

Effective teaming can incorporate a variety of models and strategies. In this model, students are highly engaged. There is less emphasis on textbooks and more on authentic and collaborative learning. Successful walking the talk strategies have long been found in elementary and middle school settings where students are involved in teaming, reading and writing workshops, science labs, and project-based learning. When partners are intentional and transparent in their collaboration, they can model in subtle but powerful ways to their students (and adults as well) that effective communication, building consensus, and problem solving are effective tools. They can also demonstrate how to appreciate and accommodate a diversity of thought and style, something that unfortunately many of our students do not see enough of these days.

The Challenges of Walking the Talk Co-Teaching

Eager but inexperienced co-teachers can easily become disheartened and burn out if their plans are too ambitious to be practical. It is best to underpromise and overdeliver on teaming until your partnership comes into its stride.

Insufficient trust in the competency of your partner or worries about maintaining the integrity of the content can become sources of unnecessary stress and eventually sabotage the partnership. Other potentially problematic issues are classroom management, levels of accountability in preparation and delivery, and insufficient planning time. Space, resource limitations, noise levels, pacing, and availability, access, and support of technology can all be potential trouble spots as well.

Without clear divisions of labor, planning, identified instructional responsibilities, and adequate timing, pacing, and directions, your efforts could be for naught. Watch for faulty assumptions about how well students can work collaboratively, problem solve, move between stations, work independently, make efficient use of time, and monitor appropriate time on task. We have come across many teachers who have not laid the groundwork to maximize this experience for their students. Once the teachers review cooperative learning strategies such as establishing group norms, providing processes for problem solving, and modeling and practicing transition periods, the students report much more rigorous learning experiences.

This model demands the most trusting partnerships, lots of communication, interdependence, sharing of all resources and expertise, and large chunks of time for planning, so be patient with your partner during this developmental process.

Walking the Talk Models in Practice

In this section, we highlight examples of how a creative walk-the-talk interdisciplinary grade-level team—in which all team members share responsibilities for teaching the core subjects—has used this model. We also feature a story about an eleventh-grade social studies teaching pair that used an oral history project as the impetus to engage students, which also served as the tipping point of their partnership's impressive development. Before you think about implementing teaming strategies like those presented here, be sure to have key elements in place such as partner trust, planning time, curricular expertise, and multiple grouping options.

Seventh-Grade Walking the Talk Co-Teaching: Teaming

A seventh-grade interdisciplinary team following a block schedule consists of Beth, a language arts teacher, Luann, a social studies teacher, Stan, a math teacher, Megan, a special education teacher, and Tom, a fine arts teacher. In addition, Paula, the paraprofessional, spends the two morning blocks supporting an identified group of seventh graders with at least one of the core teachers and the other half doing the same for the eighth-grade team.

During the fall semester, Beth, Stan, and Megan taught the following lesson to their entire block as a culmination of a short unit on symbolism, which allowed the team to meet their learning goals by collaborating in creative and unique ways using a variety of co-teaching models. Beth and Megan introduced the unit using full-class instruction, while Stan created a graphic organizer on the interactive whiteboard using vocabulary words and corresponding pictures. Then the class moved to stations: Megan facilitated an activity in which students were asked to draw picture representations of the first day of school. Luann showed pictures of symbolic images and encouraged a free-flow writing exercise about words. Tom orchestrated a collage station where students read a list of adjectives to describe themselves and then cut pictures from magazines to make self-collages. Paula, the paraeducator, helped provide IEP accommodations for two specific students the team felt would need additional support. She was also able to assist with the collage station. Stan facilitated an independent station where students used laptops from the traveling computer station. Beth was on call if an issue arose at any of the stations, but her primary task was to be the watchful observer, recorder, and facilitator. She kept the entire process moving by signaling for students to change stations at the appropriate time, and she wrote observation notes recording any difficulties students or teachers experienced as well as spontaneous reflections from all of the participants.

During the spring semester, Debbie, the school counselor, joined the team as they were planning their social studies geography unit. All of the seventh-grade students were assigned to write research papers. Luann, Beth, and Megan copresented the unit to each of the classes. The introduction included an explanation of the assignments, rubrics, and sample products from the previous year. Paula and Debbie arranged their schedules to assist in each of these classes in order to give additional support to six of the students Debbie counseled as well as Paula's assigned students. Rather than hover over their students, Paula and Debbie focused their support to increase time on task and intentional observations to check for understanding. They met regularly with the rest of the team to share insights and their comments from an observation form the team developed.

The team utilized stations (as appropriate) to help teach and reinforce writing and research skills in all of the seventh-grade classes in the few weeks leading up to the final assignment due date. The team built in opportunities for students to strengthen their cooperative learning skills and follow procedures and protocols during the collaborative team times at each of the stations. Each teacher also posted a sign-up sheet giving students the opportunity to sign up for one-on-one conferences with any one of the team members. The teachers often took turns offering small-group skill development focused on specific research tools. Independent activities at computer stations were always available and were often supported by the paraeducator and the counselor.

The team closed out the school year by teaching a career exploration course to all of the seventh graders. This course was created because of rising high school dropout rates and the district's desire to improve the percentage of students continuing their education beyond high school. The team agreed to embed the career exploration unit into the last nine-week term in required English classes. The team chose Tom as lead teacher, and the others divided up roles and responsibilities according to their own interests and passions, as opposed to the content area they usually taught.

In preparation for this unit, Debbie provided a professional development session in which she presented the team with a deeper understanding of the demands of the global workforce as well as the realities and issues facing the students in the high-poverty, culturally diverse neighborhoods their school served. The school did not have an EL teacher, even though the Hispanic population had grown significantly during the last few years, so Luann offered to translate into Spanish a program description of the upcoming career fair as well as additional resources for families.

Throughout the short but jam-packed unit, the whole team used a variety of strategies, beginning with an opening session in which they posed as potential employers and college and training admissions officers to give a short real-life experience to the students. A mini-lecture about globalization and how it is impacting the neighborhood followed, and students were responsible for sharing the notes they took with their families. The next day, students visited four stations to learn about the kinds of education and employment opportunities they might be interested in and how their choices were related to the amount of education they received. Days four through six were spent planning for mock interviews simulating experiences they might face as they apply for postsecondary education or training or employment; using community resources, Internet sites, and other primary sources; and meeting in small groups where the team coached on specific skills and knowledge. With the help of community volunteers, students took part in mock role plays for postsecondary institutions or possible employment opportunities. In the culminating activity, which lasted a few days, the students completed reflective activities and action planning that helped them make more informed decisions about their education and career choices.

In addition to the student benefits, there were positive outcomes for the teachers as well. The team increased their own skills and knowledge and enhanced their shared practice just by learning from one another. For example, because of the professional development Debbie provided to prepare the team for the unit, the faculty felt much more able to prepare their students for the challenges they will likely face in the future.

The team held a day-long debriefing session at the end of each year to determine their lessons learned and how they will help frame their plans for the coming year. They presented evidence that the high levels of student engagement from their co-taught units carried over into students' performance in more traditionally taught units. The team felt this was because of the multiple ways students were given to demonstrate mastery of the concepts and the modeling of positive relationships by the teachers and peers.

The group's ideas for rigorous and well-planned teaming units continue to grow, and the team members seem hard pressed to imagine teaching any other way. In fact, other colleagues and community leaders have volunteered ideas and offered to partner on the next big unit.

In this model of teaming, teachers are enlightened by meaningful professional conversations. Students have the opportunity to work with different teaching styles and a variety of instructional strategies to match their learning styles and abilities. Students and teachers in the example reported that the richness of tools, experiences, and products were "awesome." The team credited one another for the collective effort and accomplishments of their students. Students more easily met standards. Cooperative skills were authentic and modeled by both adults and students. Connections to prior knowledge and practical application of learning were built into lessons. And students had a variety of choices for getting the necessary support to be successful.

Eleventh-Grade Walking the Talk Co-Teaching: Teaming

On the first day of school, Dave learned that he was paired with Mary Lucia in both of his junior social studies U.S. history co-taught classes. Mary Lucia was one of the most seasoned—and resistant—of all the special education teachers in the district. Midway into the semester, Dave had a hard time justifying the time Mary Lucia spent in his room. While their doubts were unspoken, both partners felt they were foundering. They blamed their lack of effort on the fact they had been placed together with no training, no common planning time, and no real vision that co-teaching had benefits.

Then, over lunch one day, Mary Lucia casually mentioned she was interviewing her father and collecting stories of his time in the navy that she would send to the Library of Congress National Veterans History Project. Dave was immediately intrigued with the process, and he asked Mary Lucia if she would help him figure out how to incorporate oral histories for the National Veterans History Project into a standards-based unit for their students. The pair thought the project could bring history alive for their students, but they needed to decide how to embed required social studies standards and develop meaningful learning activities. Together they were able to come up with a differentiated standards-based unit plan that fit all of their students.

Once they discovered a shared passion—documenting and preserving stories of World War II veterans—the partners became fast friends. They began with a side-by-side parallel strategy, teaching each group about the protocols to use with their veterans while obtaining oral histories. They held conferencing sessions to help individuals or pairs of students identify veterans to interview. They used a whole-class mini-lecture format to model and role-play interview sessions, and they set up stations for each of the critical components of production. These stations included (1) written documentation, logs, author pages, and reflections; (2) video equipment demonstrations and instructional practices; and (3) preservation of artifacts along with veteran relations. Dave and Mary Lucia's quick but intense introduction to co-teaching was unlike the slower developmental process most typical co-teaching partners go through. This team went from an initially peaceful, but unproductive, coexistence to suddenly walking the talk. Planning time just happened because they needed a plan.

What started out as a potentially difficult year resulted in a rewarding experience for students and all the adults involved. It began with a brief but genuine exchange in which Dave asked for information on Mary Lucia's interests, and their partnership was transformed. A personal passion helped inspire Mary Lucia to overcome her reluctance to teach in a general education setting, raise the low expectations she had of her resource students, and become comfortable in the core social studies content. Dave led the effort to lay the foundation for a productive collaboration by retrofitting the partnership using critical conversations protocols. Because Dave had been involved in one of our trainings and knew about the critical conversations process, he was able to embed many of the protocols into their planning process. The students had an authentic learning opportunity connecting to community members. One of the students who was in danger of dropping out of school thanked Dave and Mary Lucia for "bringing history to life for me." He commented that he "never knew I could like learning so much." This walk the talk strategy benefited the community and brought social studies standards to life for students. Dave and Mary Lucia were quick to ask their principal if they could be paired again for the coming year. And they are already making plans to expand these strategies in other social studies units.

Summary of Co-Teaching Models

With thoughtful planning, each of the co-teaching models described here has a place and can benefit students, adults, and your professional practices. Table 2.1 lists the three models and summarizes them for quick reference.

Lessons Learned

During our coaching sessions we always ask our co-teachers to reflect on the benefits, challenges, models, and strategies they have experienced so that they can use these lessons learned to help inform future collaborations. The reflections are consistent. We have synthesized and highlighted the most important ones to close out this chapter and to help set the tone for the next chapter.

Be willing to be disturbed. Many of our colleagues refer to a protocol in Set 1 featuring an article by Margaret Wheatley (2002). Wheatley reminds us that change is difficult but inevitable. She believes that "we will succeed in changing this world only if we can think and work together in new ways. Curiosity is what we need. We don't have to let go of what we believe, but we do need to be curious of what someone else believes. We do need to acknowledge that their way of interpreting the world might be essential to our survival." She continues, "We have to be willing to admit that we're not capable of figuring things out alone" (p. 36). So get out of your comfort zone and build some trust in the process.

Table 2.1: The Three Models of Co-Teaching

Complementary Co-Teaching	Side-by-Side Co-Teaching	Walking the Talk Co-Teaching
Both teachers agree that one leads the instruction while the other teacher observes or supports individual students, small groups of students, or the co-teacher.	Both teachers take a more active role in designing instruction, grouping students, and delivering instruction. Common side-by-side groupings include one large and one smaller group, two equal groups, and multiple learning centers or stations.	Both teachers share full responsibility for all that happens in the classroom, including continuously planning, implementing, and evaluating student outcomes.

Start with the end in mind. That old adage rings true, and we are convinced of how important it is. Spend the time to do it right.

Use your passion as a motivator. Did you always want to differentiate your instruction but have never had the time? Were you curious whether multiple groupings could increase your effectiveness in reaching more of your students? Did you think it would be cool to try a textbook-less unit, but felt it was too daunting a task to try alone? Whatever your curious passion in teaching is, find a way to bring it to life collaboratively.

Set goals. Clear goals help you keep a singular shared focus on your students. Begin by setting immediate goals such as improving teaching strategies, engaging students, and finding ways to increase your planning time efficiency and effectiveness. Also make sure to have some stretch goals to help you raise your expectations of the learning that is possible in your shared classroom.

Be creative. Don't reinvent the wheel. The models and strategies are good starting points, but they are just starting points. Modify, adapt, adjust, revise, and improve to make the models your own.

Ask one another tough questions. For instance, what outcomes do we want for our students? What is the most appropriate instructional match for each of our students? How can we design roles and responsibilities to play to our strengths and minimize our challenges? How do we protect our integrity during this process? How can we help our students connect the dots to the other learning in which they are involved? How can we make this fun?

Hang tough and stay the course! Manage your expectations, because this is a developmental process. Rome wasn't built in a day, and neither is co-teaching. Get professional learning, training, and coaching. Ask peers to observe your co-teaching and provide you with feedback. Put research about quality instruction into practice.

Add value. This is not a tag-team event where you just take turns. Be able to show how valuable your contributions are—every single day. Capture measurable data that will help identify student needs and your collaborative responses. Find quantifiable and qualitative ways to demonstrate your return on investment.

Knowing the various models and strategies and referring to these lessons learned will move you to the crux of the co-teaching process in chapter 3—The Critical Conversations in Co-Teaching Framework.

3

THE CRITICAL CONVERSATIONS IN CO-TEACHING FRAMEWORK

Conversation Starters

- Why is it important to have critical conversations?
- What are the benefits of having critical conversations?
- What framework can help us to facilitate the critical conversations process?
- Will my partner and I be able to individualize our approach to critical conversations?

This chapter describes a proven process—critical conversations—to help you and your co-teacher use a problem-solving approach to move your practice forward. You can also use critical conversations to develop and strengthen other partnerships and teams in which you are a member, whether you are on a consultation team, curriculum team, grade-level, or department teams, or whether you are one of the many specialists (Title I, English learner, speech therapist, and so on).

More specifically, *critical conversations* are sets of conversation protocols—detailed activities for communication and reflection—that span the wide spectrum of exchanges that effective collaborators experience. The critical conversations protocols begin with a focus on relationship building and end by helping you and your partner ensure the necessary system supports are in place so that you can continue to grow and improve in your collaborative practice.

We developed the critical conversations as we examined stories we had collected during our work, stories such as the following:

- Very resistant teacher Mary had been teaching in her room for twenty-three years, door closed. She felt like she was being punished when she found out two days before school started that she was being paired with Sam, who she described as "that new guy fresh out of teachers' college." How could Sam really expect to add value to her classroom?

- Sarah Beth and her students with learning disabilities had been ousted from their self-contained room, only to be spread out all over the high school—surely to fail. How was she going to be able to work with different teachers every period? And besides, she was a "special teacher" by choice. She didn't know content! How could her principal possibly expect her to teach high school courses?

- Barry had taught freshman algebra courses for several years, always making heroic efforts to modify and adapt lessons for struggling students while his co-teacher, Wilma, milled around, often reading the newspaper or checking her email during class. How could he truthfully respond if asked about her professionalism or the contributions she was making to his class?

- What about Alex and Maya, the speech pathologist and the English language teacher? Could co-teaching finally allow them to be seen as valued colleagues who could help support students while in their general education classrooms?

In all of these situations, the educators found ways to work together to add value for their students through co-teaching. These examples and hundreds more from teachers and administrators have convinced us that students have been better served when general and special educators (and in many cases other specialists) collaborate and plan together.

These protocols help ensure the alignment of your and your partner's beliefs about fairness, equity, parity, shared resources, and ethical responsibilities. All collaborative partners have different skills, knowledge, and abilities, enabling them to add their unique and valuable contributions to their co-teaching. These planned critical conversations can help ensure that the co-teaching experience offers students more than what either co-teacher could provide to students alone.

Because co-teachers' commitments are to the students for whom they share responsibility, they will jointly design, implement, and evaluate substantive instruction. They are not bound to content alone, or to the assigned students with special needs, or to the place where they do their work. When co-teachers enter into a co-teaching relationship, they must make decisions together that will be influenced by their individual expertise and style, the content they must teach, and the space and resources available to them—in addition to the makeup of the classroom, data on student achievement and needs, scheduling issues, and available planning times. These are all considerations in determining the best co-teaching models to use during instruction. Once built, a partnership can be fluid and flexible in adjusting and modifying co-teaching models based on the demands of the students, the adults, and the curriculum.

Whether co-teaching is used to address a districtwide school improvement effort or meet legislative mandates, or it results from an action research project, there is real benefit in encouraging co-teachers to become teacher-leaders who can demonstrate co-teaching models, articulate the benefits, problem-solve the challenges, support increased accountability with data, and advocate collaborative practices as powerful instructional strategies for meeting the needs of a diverse student body. Indeed, we have witnessed situations where co-teaching started as a small but critical mass and became the catalyst for massive schoolwide improvements. The return on investment you can expect for your students will be maximized when you have intentional conversations about these factors.

Margaret Wheatley (2005) writes, "It takes courage to start a conversation. But if we don't start talking to one another, nothing will change. Conversation is the way we discover how to transform our world, together" (p. 27). Our passionate belief is that there is no better way to change our school community than by talking to one another. Critical conversations strengthen collaborations with others who share responsibility for the same students and who care deeply about improving student success.

Whether you are teaching with one partner for a single class period or have a whole team of collaborators throughout the day, we can almost guarantee your efforts will improve when you work together using critical conversations to strengthen your communication. So what kind of communication are we talking about?

Often talk between teachers is no more than having a quick chat in the hall on the way to another class or stopping long enough to review the next day's lesson plan. But when partners talk intentionally about themselves and their work, they enhance their collaboration. Teachers gain a much deeper appreciation for one another's contributions, suggest ways to maximize strengths, shore up differences, analyze student needs, find appropriate instructional matches to student needs, and successfully solve problems when they communicate in deeper ways. Effective collaboration can lead to a return on investment measured in increased student engagement, more focused instruction, enhanced relationships, decreased student behavior issues, and improved student learning. In the end, it is not so much about the common planning time we have or don't have. It's about what we talk about when we do talk.

The Critical Conversations Framework

The critical conversations framework is divided into four sets of protocols gleaned from our work with educators:

1 Critical Conversations to Engage Partners

2 Critical Conversations to Examine Data

3 Critical Conversations to Enhance Instruction

4 Critical Conversations to Expand Impact

Critical Conversations Protocol Format and Priorities

Each conversation set begins by asking key focus questions to help guide your thinking. Each conversation set includes protocols—the directions for activities that will help facilitate your conversations. These protocols contain a variety of activities designed to help you and your partner in the following broad areas:

- Relationship building
- Processing
- Reflecting
- Advocating
- Assessing
- Planning
- Goal setting

The wide variety of text-based protocols includes activities, templates, and surveys. While many of them would be beneficial if used by individual teachers, they were designed to be used collaboratively with a partner or team. Each set also includes anticipated outcomes. When you are able to answer the anticipated outcomes with solid evidence, you can assume you are ready to move forward to a new protocol.

To determine which protocols you and your partner or team will work through, refer to the Reflective Journal (page 46), and discuss each of the focus questions. These focus questions will give you an idea of the content of each protocol.

Each set of critical conversations is prioritized according to importance: whether they are crucial, relate to special occasions, or involve those conversations that we always hope to have time for and seldom do.

Non-Negotiable Conversations

We begin with *non-negotiable conversations*—the conversations we recommend above all others. These protocols appear in the beginning of each conversation set and provide a minimum foundation for collaborative work. The sooner these conversations take place in the relationship, the smoother your journey will be. We have seen many partnerships destroyed when partners have failed to allow the necessary time to form a solid foundation. Unspoken and unresolved issues do not get better with time. In fact, they get more difficult to bring up the longer you wait. They are like that little grain of sand in your shoe. It is hardly noticeable for the first few steps, but the longer you have to contend with it, the bigger it grows, and pretty soon you wonder how such a large stone got into your footwear. The longer you wait, the more difficult removing it becomes.

Teachers usually demonstrate a greater appreciation for their colleagues when they spend time learning about one another through these initial conversations. Teachers say that these intentional conversations have helped them discover some interesting things about their colleagues with whom they have taught for many years, but never really had the opportunity to get to know. What we learn about working with one another can help inform our shared practices.

Special Occasion Conversations

Special occasion conversations take place when you and your partner are at a critical juncture or decision point concerning your collaboration. Different situations call for different strategies. You will find some of these relevant for your situation and others not.

In a Perfect World Conversations

In a perfect world conversations are similar to the enrichment activities you might assign to high-achieving students to ensure they continue to be meaningfully engaged. These final conversations provide stretch opportunities to help you continue to increase your engagement and allow you to apply your expertise in new and creative ways. The time you put into these conversations is precious and hard to come by, but they can extend your collaboration beyond what most teaching partnerships are able to do.

Set 1: Critical Conversations to Engage Partners

Establishing a strong professional partnership is essential if you and your colleagues are to find common ground in the many situations you will face daily in your shared classrooms. Before you choose co-teaching models, and certainly before you determine lesson goals and design lesson plans, you and your partners will need to lay a solid foundation. This first set of conversations allows you to clarify your professional stance, come to a common understanding about your core values, and discuss what you both believe about educating all students. Then you will need to come to consensus about whose responsibility it is to educate the students you share, the expectations you have for their learning, how you will share your expertise and resources, and your commitment to ensuring student success. It won't really matter if you share resources, space, and even planning time if you both hold vastly different expectations for student learning or if you differ in the lengths you will go to ensure success for all students.

An effective shared practice must be open to questioning, confirming, and reconfirming that you and your partners share the same vision and goals, that you are committed to applying sufficient time and resources to be productive together, and also that you have the knowledge, skills, and time required to achieve the desired results. Shared vision includes a commitment to being accountable to one another as well as to your students. Once you agree on the vision and commitment you have for your students, you can determine the roles and responsibilities you will share and how you will meet the challenges that lie ahead.

Again refer to the Reflective Journal, figure 3.1 (page 46). Discussing these questions with your partner will give you a baseline on where you stand on this particular set of conversations. If you are unsure of how you feel about each of these, you have your starting point to get to the outcomes. If you can agree that you have solid evidence that you have worked through the outcomes presented, you can move on.

Following are the focus questions to self-assess your partnership:

- What do we need to talk about to develop our professional relationship?
- How can we create a shared vision for all students?
- How can we address the practicalities of our partnership?
- How can we develop agreement on the roles and responsibilities for our partnership?

It's time to move on when you have achieved these anticipated outcomes:

- We have begun conversations to develop our collaborative professional relationship.
- We have developed a shared vision for all of our students.
- We have developed agreements on the practicalities of our partnership.
- We have developed an agreement on the roles and responsibilities for our partnership.

The critical conversations activities for each of the three types of protocols in set 1 are listed in table 3.1 (page 42). The complete activities appear in chapter 6, beginning on page 79.

Set 2: Critical Conversations to Examine Data

All too often teachers jump right into making decisions about the co-teaching models and strategies they plan to use without allowing for setting of appropriate goals and joint planning of instruction. This second set of conversations will enable you to understand not only your students and their families, but also the culture of your school and community and both the supports and challenges that affect your co-teaching practice. As you gain these understandings, you will be able to set appropriate learning goals for your students.

Following are the focus questions to self-assess your partnership:

- What assumptions do we have about our students?
- What relevant school data do we have?
- How can relevant data inform our practice?

Table 3.1: Protocols for Set 1—Critical Conversations to Engage Partners

Non-Negotiable Conversations
• Building a Relationship—Relationship-Building Protocol • Sharing a Vision—Relationship-Building Protocol • Pondering the Practicalities—Processing Protocol • Determining Roles, Responsibilities, and Processes—Processing Protocol
Special Occasion Conversations
• Setting Our Norms—Processing Protocol • Getting the DIRT on One Another—Relationship-Building Protocol • Solving Our Problems—Processing Protocol • Managing Our Conflicts—Relationship-Building Protocol • Talking About Identity and Integrity—Reflecting Protocol • Being Willing to Be Disturbed—Reflecting Protocol • Getting Fierce—Communicating Protocol
In a Perfect World Conversations
• Sharing Our Personal Bests—Relationship-Building Protocol • Deciding Whether to Intervene—Assessing Protocol • Stopping the Conflict Before It Begins—Processing Protocol • Getting Ready to Co-Teach—Planning Protocol • Reflecting—Reflecting Protocol • Talking About Our Talking—Processing Protocol

- How can we set SMARTER goals to help us meet the diverse instructional needs of and improve achievement for all of our students?

It's time to move on when you have achieved these anticipated outcomes:

- We have clarified our assumptions about our students.
- We have obtained sufficient student and school data.
- We have a process to use relevant data to inform our practice.
- We have set SMARTER goals to help us meet the diverse instructional needs of and improve achievement for all of our students.

The critical conversations activities for each of the three types of protocols in set 2 are listed in table 3.2. The complete activities appear in chapter 7, beginning on page 105.

Set 3: Critical Conversations to Enhance Instruction

As partners build trust and have a deeper understanding of their students and the school community, they are ready to develop plans to support their students. The conversations in set 3 will help you decide how to use a variety of co-teaching models based on the instructional needs of students and

Table 3.2: Protocols for Set 2—Critical Conversations to Examine Data

Non-Negotiable Conversations
• Moving Beyond Assumptions—Assessing Protocol
• Having Picture Day at School—Assessing Protocol
• Committing—Goal-Setting Protocol
• Setting SMARTER Goals—Goal-Setting Protocol
Special Occasion Conversations
• Asking Our Families—Assessing Protocol
• Having a World Café for Student Voices—Assessing Protocol
• Setting Professional and Personal Goals—Goal-Setting Protocol
• Prioritizing Our Co-Teaching Characteristics—Planning Protocol
• Asking Twenty Questions—Planning Protocol
In a Perfect World Conversations
• Talking About Responsibility—Assessing Protocol
• Using Metaphors and Models That Engage Students—Planning Protocol
• Getting to Consensus: A Consensogram—Assessing Protocol

the strengths of your partnership, and will provide options for incorporating research-based practices into your co-teaching. These protocols will help you collaborate in making meaningful choices about your daily practice so that you are able to align your instructional content, context, and processes with curriculum goals and assessments.

Following are the focus questions to self-assess your partnership:

- How will we employ co-teaching models that are matched to the instructional needs of our students?

- How will we use co-teaching models to align our instructional content with standards, curriculum goals, and assessment?

- How can we incorporate evidence-based practices into our co-teaching efforts?

- How do we align our practice with professional standards and other district initiatives, such as differentiated instruction (DI), universal design for learning (UDL), professional learning communities (PLCs), response to intervention (RTI), and so on?

It's time to move on when you have achieved these anticipated outcomes:

- We understand and are able to use a variety of co-teaching models based on the instructional needs of our students.

- Our co-teaching practice matches co-teaching models to our instructional content (with standards, curriculum goals, and assessment).

- We incorporate evidenced-based practices into our co-teaching efforts.

- We align our practice with professional standards and other district initiatives, such as differentiated instruction (DI), universal design for learning (UDL), professional learning communities (PLCs), response to intervention (RTI), and so on.

The critical conversations activities for each of the three types of protocols in set 3 are listed in table 3.3. The complete activities appear in chapter 8, beginning on page 121.

Set 4: Critical Conversations to Expand Impact

Once co-teaching partnerships are well established, it is natural for these partners, along with their administrators, to consider ways in which collaborative practices can be expanded and supported throughout a school or district.

Following are the focus questions to self-assess your partnership:

- How can we continue to grow and develop our collaborative practice?

- Why, how, and when should we be communicating with others?

- How might we build and sustain individual and organizational capacity and support for our collaborative work?

- How can we recognize and acknowledge our successful collaborative efforts?

It's time to move on when you have achieved these anticipated outcomes:

- We have developed and implemented a standards-based professional growth plan to support our continued learning.

Table 3.3: Protocols for Set 3—Critical Conversations to Enhance Instruction

Non-Negotiable Conversations
• Adding Value With Co-Teaching—Planning Protocol • Value-Added Co-Teaching—Planning Protocol • Co-Teaching Alignment—Planning Protocol • Having an Accountability Chat—Reflecting Protocol
Special Occasion Conversations
• Aligning With Evidence-Based Practices—Assessing Protocol • Aligning With Differentiated Instruction (DI)—Aligning Protocol • Aligning With Universal Design for Differentiated Instruction (UDDI)—Planning Protocol • Responding to Response to Intervention (RTI)—Planning Protocol • Inviting Marzano Into Our Conversations—Planning Protocol • Considering Cultural Competence—Aligning Protocol • Aligning With Global Competence—Aligning Protocol • Observing Co-Teaching—Assessing Protocol
In a Perfect World Conversation
• Aligning With Professional Teaching Standards—Aligning Protocol

- We have developed and implemented a comprehensive communication plan to actively engage and nurture all necessary stakeholders.

- We have taken steps to build and sustain individual and organizational capacity by sharing expertise with others and adding to the collective wealth of our system.

- We have actively recognized and rewarded the collaborative successes we have experienced.

The critical conversations activities for each of the three types of protocols in set 4 are listed in table 3.4. The complete activities appear in chapter 9, beginning on page 141.

Table 3.4: Protocols for Set 4—Critical Conversations to Expand Impact

Non-Negotiable Conversations
• Growing Together—Planning Protocol
• Talking With Our Partners—Communicating Protocol
• Building Capacity—Sustaining Protocol
• Celebrating, Recognizing, and Acknowledging Our Successes—Reflecting Protocol
Special Occasion Conversations
• Going for Maximum Impact: Putting PD Into Action—Planning Protocol
• Taking Charge of Our Concerns—Communicating Protocol
• Professionalizing Our Professional Development—Planning Protocol
• Making Our Work More Meaningful—Planning Protocol
• Expanding Our Collaborations—Planning Protocol
• Strengthening Our Support—Sustaining Protocol
• Starting and Stopping Smartly—Planning Protocol
In a Perfect World Conversations
• Improving Our Expansion Efforts—Planning Protocol
• Getting Into the Policy Arena—Sustaining Protocol
• Growing Our Own Teacher Leaders—Sustaining Protocol
• Aligning With National Standards of Quality Professional Development—Planning Protocol

Preassessment and Action Plan

Again, we refer you to the Reflective Journal (fig. 3.1, page 46) to help you and your partner assess your progress as you work through the critical conversations framework and create an action plan. (Visit **go.solution-tree.com/specialneeds** to download this reproducible journal and other materials associated with this book.) It contains the focus questions and anticipated outcomes for each set, along with space to plan which conversation protocols you want to work through with your partner. As you assess your place in the framework, make decisions about the specific conversation protocols in which you will engage. When you have successfully reached the outcomes after working through the conversation protocols, mark the date of completion on your journal, and plan your further actions.

The Critical Conversations Overview (fig. 3.2, pages 48–51) lists all the conversation protocols in each set, matched with the focus questions and anticipated outcomes. Use this chart as an overview of the complete framework as you choose which critical conversations you and your partner or team will work through. It also contains page numbers so you can easily locate each critical conversation protocol within this chapter.

Figure 3.1: Reflective journal.

Focus Questions	Critical Conversation Protocol Choices	Anticipated Outcomes	Date of Completion and Further Actions
Set 1: Engage Partners			
What do we need to talk about to develop our professional relationship?		We have begun conversations to develop our collaborative professional relationship.	
How can we create a shared vision for all students?		We have developed a shared vision for all of our students.	
How can we address the practicalities of our partnership?		We have developed agreements on the practicalities of our partnership.	
How can we develop agreement on the roles and responsibilities for our partnership?		We have developed an agreement on the roles and responsibilities for our partnership.	
Set 2: Examine Data			
What assumptions do we have about our students?		We have clarified our assumptions about our students.	
What relevant school data do we have?		We have obtained sufficient student and school data.	
How can relevant data inform our practice?		We have a process to use relevant data to inform our practice.	
How can we set SMARTER goals to help us meet the diverse instructional needs of and improve achievement for all of our students?		We have set SMARTER goals to help us meet the diverse instructional needs of and improve achievement for all of our students.	
Set 3: Enhance Instruction			
How will we employ co-teaching models that are matched to the instructional needs of our students?		We understand and are able to use a variety of co-teaching models based on the instructional needs of our students.	

Focus Questions	Critical Conversation Protocol Choices	Anticipated Outcomes	Date of Completion and Further Actions
Set 3: Enhance Instruction			
How will we use co-teaching models to align our instructional content with standards, curriculum goals, and assessment?		Our co-teaching practice matches co-teaching models to our instructional content (with standards, curriculum goals, and assessment).	
How can we incorporate evidence-based practices into our co-teaching efforts?		We incorporate evidence-based practices into our co-teaching efforts.	
How do we align our practice with professional standards and other district initiatives, such as differentiated instruction (DI), universal design for learning (UDL), professional learning communities (PLCs), response to intervention (RTI), and so on?		We align our practice with professional standards and other district initiatives, such as differentiated instruction (DI), universal design for learning (UDL), professional learning communities (PLCs), response to intervention (RTI), and so on.	
Set 4: Expand Impact			
How can we continue to grow and develop our collaborative practice?		We have developed and implemented a standards-based professional growth plan to support our continued learning.	
Why, how, and when should we be communicating with others?		We have developed and implemented a comprehensive communication plan to actively engage and nurture all necessary stakeholders.	
How might we build and sustain individual and organizational capacity and support for our collaborative work?		We have taken steps to build and sustain individual and organizational capacity by sharing expertise with others and adding to the collective wealth of our system.	
How can we recognize and acknowledge our successful collaborative efforts?		We have actively recognized and rewarded the collaborative successes we have experienced.	

Visit **go.solution-tree.com/specialneeds** to download and print this figure.

Figure 3.2: Critical conversations overview.

Focus Questions	Anticipated Outcomes	Set 1: Critical Conversations to Engage Partners		
		Non-Negotiable Conversations	Special Occasion Conversations	In a Perfect World Conversations
What do we need to talk about to develop our professional relationship?	We have begun conversations to develop our collaborative professional relationship.	Building a Relationship—Relationship-Building Protocol *Page 80*	Setting Our Norms—Processing Protocol *Page 85*	Sharing Our Personal Bests—Relationship-Building Protocol *Page 99*
How can we create a shared vision for all students?	We have developed a shared vision for all of our students.	Sharing a Vision—Relationship-Building Protocol *Page 81*	Getting the DIRT on One Another—Relationship-Building Protocol *Page 86*	Deciding Whether to Intervene—Assessing Protocol *Page 99*
How can we address the practicalities of our partnership?	We have developed agreements on the practicalities of our partnership.	Pondering The Practicalities—Processing Protocol *Page 82*	Solving Our Problems—Processing Protocol *Page 90*	Stopping the Conflict Before It Begins—Processing Protocol *Page 100*
How can we develop agreement on the roles and responsibilities for our partnership?	We have developed an agreement on the roles and responsibilities for our partnership.	Determining Roles, Responsibilities, and Processes—Processing Protocol *Page 84*	Managing Our Conflicts—Relationship-Building Protocol *Page 92*	Getting Ready to Co-Teach—Planning Protocol *Page 100*
			Talking About Identity and Integrity—Reflecting Protocol *Page 93*	Reflecting—Reflecting Protocol *Page 103*
			Being Willing to Be Disturbed—Reflecting Protocol *Page 95*	Talking About Our Talking—Processing Protocol *Page 103*
			Getting Fierce—Communicating Protocol *Page 98*	

Focus Questions	Anticipated Outcomes	Non-Negotiable Conversations	Special Occasion Conversations	In a Perfect World Conversations
Set 2: Critical Conversations to Examine Data				
What assumptions do we have about our students?	We have clarified our assumptions about our students.	Moving Beyond Assumptions—Assessing Protocol _Page 106_	_Asking Our Families—Assessing Protocol_ _Page 111_	Talking About Responsibility—Assessing Protocol _Page 117_
What relevant school data do we have?	We have obtained sufficient student and school data.	Having Picture Day at School—Assessing Protocol _Page 106_	Having a World Café for Student Voices—Assessing Protocol _Page 112_	Using Metaphors and Models That Engage Students—Planning Protocol _Page 118_
How can relevant data inform our practice?	We have a process to use relevant data to inform our practice.			
How can we set SMARTER goals to help us meet the diverse instructional needs of and improve achievement for all of our students?	We have set SMARTER goals to help us meet the diverse instructional needs of and improve achievement for all of our students.	Committing—Goal-Setting Protocol _Page 109_	Setting Professional and Personal Goals—Goal-Setting Protocol _Page 113_	Getting to Consensus: A Consensogram—Assessing Protocol _Page 119_
		Setting SMARTER Goals—Goal-Setting Protocol _Page 109_	Prioritizing Our Co-Teaching Characteristics—Planning Protocol _Page 113_	
			Asking Twenty Questions—Planning Protocol _Page 115_	
Set 3: Critical Conversations to Enhance Instruction				
How will we employ co-teaching models that are matched to the instructional needs of our students?	We understand and are able to use a variety of co-teaching models based on the instructional needs of our students.	Adding Value With Co-Teaching—Planning Protocol _Page 122_	Aligning With Evidence-Based Practices—Assessing Protocol _Page 126_	Aligning With Professional Teaching Standards—Aligning Protocol _Page 138_
How will we use co-teaching models to align our instructional content with standards, curriculum goals, and assessment?	Our co-teaching practice matches co-teaching models to our instructional content (with standards, curriculum goals, and assessment).	Value-Added Co-Teaching—Planning Protocol _Page 123_	Aligning With Differentiated Instruction (DI)—Aligning Protocol _Page 127_	
		Co-Teaching Alignment—Planning Protocol _Page 125_	Aligning With Universal Design for Differentiated Instruction (UDDI)—Planning Protocol _Page 128_	

continued →

Set 3: Critical Conversations to Enhance Instruction

Focus Questions	Anticipated Outcomes	Non-Negotiable Conversations	Special Occasion Conversations	In a Perfect World Conversations
How can we incorporate evidence-based practices into our co-teaching efforts?	We incorporate evidenced-based practices into our co-teaching efforts.	Having an Accountability Chat—Reflecting Protocol *Page 125*	Responding to Response to Intervention (RTI)—Planning Protocol *Page 129*	
How do we align our practice with professional standards and other district initiatives, such as differentiated instruction (DI), universal design for learning (UDL), professional learning communities (PLCs), response to intervention (RTI), and so on?	We align our practice with professional standards and other district initiatives, such as differentiated instruction (DI), universal design for learning (UDL), professional learning communities (PLCs), response to intervention (RTI), and so on.		Inviting Marzano Into Our Conversations—Planning Protocol *Page 130* Considering Cultural Competence—Aligning Protocol *Page 132* Aligning With Global Competence—Aligning Protocol *Page 133* Observing Co-Teaching—Assessing Protocol *Page 135*	

Set 4: Critical Questions to Expand Impact

Focus Questions	Anticipated Outcomes	Non-Negotiable Conversations	Special Occasion Conversations	In a Perfect World Conversations
How can we continue to grow and develop our collaborative practice?	We have developed and implemented a standards-based professional growth plan to support our continued learning.	Growing Together—Planning Protocol *Page 142*	Going for Maximum Impact: Putting PD Into Action—Planning Protocol *Page 146*	Improving Our Expansion Efforts—Planning Protocol *Page 155*
Why, how, and when should we be communicating with others?	We have developed and implemented a comprehensive communication plan to actively engage and nurture all necessary stakeholders.	Talking With Our Partners—Communicating Protocol *Page 143*	Taking Charge of Our Concerns—Communicating Protocol *Page 147*	Getting Into the Policy Arena—Sustaining Protocol *Page 156*
How might we build and sustain individual and organizational capacity and support for our collaborative work?		Building Capacity—Sustaining Protocol *Page 143*	Professionalizing Our Professional Development—Planning Protocol *Page 149*	Growing Our Own Teacher Leaders—Sustaining Protocol *Page 157*

Set 4: Critical Questions to Expand Impact

Focus Questions	Anticipated Outcomes	Non-Negotiable Conversations	Special Occasion Conversations	In a Perfect World Conversations
How can we recognize and acknowledge our successful collaborative efforts?	We have taken steps to build and sustain individual and organizational capacity by sharing expertise with others and adding to the collective wealth of our system. We have actively recognized and rewarded the collaborative successes we have experienced.	Celebrating, Recognizing, and Acknowledging Our Successes—Reflecting Protocol *Page 145*	Making Our Work More Meaningful—Planning Protocol *Page 151* Expanding Our Collaborations—Planning Protocol *Page 152* Strengthening Our Support—Sustaining Protocol *Page 153* Starting and Stopping Smartly—Planning Protocol *Page 154*	Aligning With National Standards of Quality Professional Development—Planning Protocol *Page 157*

*Visit **go.solution-tree.com/specialneeds** to download and print this figure.*

Summary: Start Talking

Our hope is that you will accept our invitation, invite your partners, and use our critical conversations framework to improve your co-teaching efforts. The detailed critical conversation protocols themselves appear in chapters 6, 7, 8, and 9. Some of them have been adapted from the work of well-known educators and authors. They include step-by-step activities, templates, tools, and other resources. There are no suggested time limits for the conversations. Some partners or teams might spend considerable time on the early-stage conversations as they build a solid foundation; others go straight to a problem-solving protocol that seems relevant to their situation.

Now that you have a basic understanding about the framework and the kinds of conversation protocols that you will find in each step, we move to chapter 4, which offers you a glimpse into how this process looks in action. You will meet teachers like yourself who are learning to work more efficiently and effectively to help their students improve, and they are doing this by using critical conversations.

CRITICAL CONVERSATIONS IN ACTION

Conversation Starters

- How did these co-teaching teams develop a shared vision for all students? What might our shared vision be?

- What do these examples show about using data to inform practice? How do we use our data in co-teaching?

- What co-teaching strategies and approaches improved these co-teaching teams and their instructional plans? How might we use a variety of strategies and approaches for instruction?

- How do these examples show their continuous addition of value to instructional design and implementation? What might add value with our instruction and co-teaching implementation?

Now that we have given you a preview of the four sets of critical conversations and the protocols for each set, we offer some stories from real teachers that illustrate co-teaching in action. Co-teaching is something like learning to swim. You can execute all of the right strokes, remember to breathe, and actually stay afloat, but you may not feel like a real swimmer until you can get out there and swim with the sharks.

The following stories show how the critical conversations in co-teaching framework functions in a variety of contexts, at various skill levels, and with different challenges. The stories are composites of educators we have had the privilege of working with over the years. In the end, all of these partners have found ways to embed the concepts found in this book into meaningful professional development in their daily practice while enhancing learning opportunities for their students.

As you read these stories, you will see evidence of many of the elements experienced teachers list as essential for successful co-teaching. Administrative support is always close to the top of everyone's list, which typically includes such things as understanding, patience, and a willingness to allow risk-taking as teachers experiment with collaboration and co-teaching. Other factors that contribute positively to collaboration and co-teaching include trust and respect from colleagues; a respectful and structured planning time focused on making good instructional matches; a solid relationship built on good communication; quality professional development that includes follow-up coaching; and establishing shared commitments. In the places where co-teaching is successful, it is a priority and there is professional respect for all special and general educators, other specialists, and teaching assistants.

Chapter 5, "Expanding Co-Teaching Conversations," investigates set 4 in greater detail. It explores what happens once partners and teams have established critical conversations and co-teachers and administrators wish to spread the wealth to other colleagues in a more systemic approach to the implementation of co-teaching.

Each co-teaching team's story highlights various aspects of the critical conversations framework that you will learn about in more depth in chapters 6–9. The protocols have been used specifically by teachers in similar situations to those illustrated here as we worked together in improving and enhancing their co-teaching conversations and ultimate practice.

The First Pancake

We begin with a pair of middle school teachers who started their process of implementing co-teaching strategies out of genuine concern for their students and their relationship with one another. While they did have administrative support, one of their biggest challenges was the feeling they were lone rangers in a school that was slow to adapt inclusive practices. They attributed this feeling to their belief that they held higher expectations for all of their students, especially those with special needs, than many of their colleagues. After finding their own way, they are now committed to spreading their enthusiasm for collaborative practices.

Melissa and Jen are two bright young middle school teachers in a struggling urban school. Melissa quickly became chair of the English department because of her strong organizational and leadership skills. Her classroom is across the hall from Jen, the popular and highly energetic special educator assigned to teach several self-contained resource rooms at the middle school. Because Jen's students have a range of needs from learning disabilities to more intense needs, she often went across the hall to pick Melissa's brain about how she used differentiated instruction strategies and multiple groupings in her English classes.

Jen and Melissa's partnership began three years ago in an attempt to improve state test scores in each of their classes. They shared "track time" burning off calories before school each morning on laps around the high school track. They learned they shared similar planning and teaching processes, and by spring they approached Principal Hall to see if they could combine some of their classes to maximize their efforts.

There were no co-teachers in their building, and neither Jen nor Melissa had co-teaching experience, so they weren't sure how to begin. They did, however, have a few very important things going for them: they were both good teachers, they had a solid personal relationship and professional trust and respect as colleagues, and they were fearless. Principal Hall gave them a common planning time and the flexibility to move their classes in and out of their rooms—as long as they could tell her their instructional goals and how the strategies would help students. They began by reading a couple of textbooks on co-teaching, but reading about doing something didn't seem to work for the team.

So to get a feel for one another's roles and responsibilities, they created their own reality show—Jen for the Day, Melissa for the Day—switching roles with each other one day in the late spring. By expanding her understanding of special education, writing IEPs, going to case conferences, and dealing with issues of students with more significant needs, Melissa came away with a greater appreciation of all of the tasks special educators have to perform in addition to their teaching duties.

Jen gained a whole new appreciation for general education, including the depth of content knowledge required in general education and the importance of having regular routines and procedures for dealing with larger groups of students. Her heart sank when she admitted feeling she had been watering down her curricula, and when she did have larger groups of students, her behavior procedures amounted to little more than crowd control.

Trading days with one another helped them be much more realistic when they divided up their partnership roles and responsibilities. During a summer institute, they learned about collaboration, co-teaching models, and strategies.

The pair was able to dig deeper into data on their students for the coming year. They added reviewing and disaggregating the results of the school's state test results to the list of all of the ways they could assess their students' interests, aptitudes, and learning preferences.

They committed to making preassessments a hallmark of their collaborations, administering them before introducing any new material and at other critical times. Because many of the students struggled with difficult home lives, Jen and Melissa created a welcoming letter letting families know they would be co-teaching and listing the many benefits they anticipated for their students as a result.

They spent the rest of the summer looking over the middle school standards that applied to the required English content, choosing three units to co-teach during the fall semester. They had fun rearranging the physical space and realized that the climate and setting they were creating would facilitate effective community building.

Jen and Melissa's planning for the units was adapted from Tomlinson and McTighe's model for differentiated instruction and began with a Know, Understand, and Do template that included anticipated outcomes, essential questions, learning activities, and assessments. They embedded specific co-teaching strategies into their learning activities.

As Jen recalled, "Yeah, that lasted a short time; we felt like the delivery was too stiff and artificial, so we were soon teaming in all of our classes. The synergy really began to take off when we abandoned 'by the book' models. We do still use them in our planning—but more like guideposts and to help keep us on track."

Principal Hall reported that many students, parents, and even newer colleagues forgot who the general educator was and who the special educator was in this pair. Jen and Melissa have noticeably reduced behavior problems, and student engagement is at an all-time high. The students with IEPs improved their percentages in almost all of their English standard components. Scores were significantly higher than they had been for this group during the three previous years. The students without IEPs had also shown higher gains than any other English class in the building. Their results alleviated one of the principal's early concerns about whether or not the shared classes would have a detrimental effect on all of the other students.

The only challenge they continued to struggle with was a phenomenon they called "integrity or activity?"—getting so caught up in their own fun (using props and costumes to illustrate literary work, performing skits, doing kooky things) that all of a sudden they'd notice they'd left the kids behind.

Word spread that Principal Hall had created an inclusion plan to move more students out of resource rooms and into general education rooms, a change that would affect several students, three additional resource room special educators, six general educators, two in math, and teachers in social studies and science. Ms. Hall used a differentiated approach with her staff much as a good teacher would with her students. She carefully selected when and how to bring additional teachers on board. She developed a communications plan, informing all of the stakeholders of possible changes and providing ways to involve them in the process. And as Melissa recalled:

> She told everyone about making her "first pancake"—you know, the one that you make to check if the consistency of the batter and the heat are okay. To her, the first pancake was our attempt to do something that doesn't quite measure up, even though you know how to make it and you have all of the right ingredients. Ms. Hall was fond of saying that if you persevere, you continue to improve on that first pancake until you get the results you want. She allowed us the time to show results. We tried lots of things that first year, and it kept getting better, just like the pancakes do.

As they began their fourth year together, Jen reflected on the experience this way:

> As I think about it, I am much more organized and rigorous in all of my work as a result of working so closely with Melissa, and she, well, she brings a lot more of herself to her practice. We *were* both good teachers, but when we look back, we were both sort of floating over the curriculum, our data, and our competence. As we began to incorporate meaningful conversations into our relationship, we were able to go much deeper. Now we're really diving in. Ms. Hall even calls Melissa and me school leaders!

Taylor's Story

Taylor taught sixth grade in a small rural community. He graciously shared this story of a metamorphosis that happened to his sixth graders and the special educator with whom he taught.

> I had been a trainer in the corporate world before making a decision to become a teacher. Returning to college, I soaked up educational theory and evidence-based practices. I knew I could teach well and my students would learn. I held some pretty strong predispositions. I'm sorry to admit that I once believed that special students, the ones with difficult academic or behavior challenges, they were the students who could keep me from teaching the ones I was meant to teach. Seems so funny to hear that now, but I really thought there was a group of students that I didn't want to be a distraction to what I was doing in the classroom. I knew I could send them down the hall to the resource room.
>
> My experiences with "those kids" began the first day of my student-teaching placement. The special educator walked into my general education room and laid down the law. She told me and my supervising teacher that we could not grade, punish, or provide consequences to any of "her students" for their actions in the classroom. Whenever issues arose, her students were free to leave my classroom and meet with her in the resource room. When they were in my class, I was to help them and give them at least fifteen to twenty extra minutes to complete assignments. They were free to go to the resource room to have directions and tests read to them.
>
> This was not my idea of collaboration. My supervising teacher and I were shocked, my feelings were bruised, and then I became more defensive of my practice. While I saw this

as a challenge, this was not a collaborative environment. I did nothing with the identified kids. When instructional aides appeared sporadically, we never knew what they were doing with the students, and it seemed to me that this special educator was more like the police making sure that I gave her students all of the benefits with no expectations that they could do any of the work.

When I began my actual teaching career in a sixth-grade classroom at a neighboring school, I felt pretty good about my attempts to reach all of my assigned students, and appreciative that I only had a few students with special needs. The special educators helped with modifications and accommodations and also followed up in the resource room the last period of the day. Not a great plan, but it seemed to work.

I was getting into a real groove, feeling confident—that is, until my third year. I had heard about Jeremy Johnson when I came to the school. Much to my surprise, I finally understood why teachers got depressed when they had to deal with him. Jeremy had a history of violence, not just with students but with teachers as well. He was going to be too disruptive to my "real" students, so I marched down to the office pleading with administration and asking how they could do that to me. Clearly the school administrators knew how well my students had scored on state achievement tests. They had bragged about how I was able to move my students from below to average and above on all of our high-stakes tests. I was a really good teacher, and now they were going to bring some kid in to destroy all of that.

Delores, Jeremy's special education teacher, was in my room for half of the day to support him. I didn't like it, but at least Delores didn't interfere or judge how I was handling this deplorable situation. I worked more overtime than usual during the first three weeks of school to overcome this terrible predicament. Then, during an incredible science lesson, the train wreck happened. Jeremy caused complete chaos to erupt in my class with his noisy outbursts, and I rushed through the lesson as quickly as I could. Delores was nice enough, even helpful, but all I could see was a snapshot of what Jeremy was doing to interfere with my teaching.

Delores had been teaching for over twenty years; she was a well-respected and quite conservative community member, and being new to this community, I was always guarded in my conversations and certainly fought to hold my emotions in check. I was mad not only at Jeremy, but at the school principal who placed him in my class, at Delores for her "special-ness," at the laws that allowed this to happen, and at myself for being so angry. And naïvely perhaps, I tried hard to stay calm on the outside, believing that Delores wouldn't pick up on my anger and frustration. In addition to my own initial resistance, there were lots of questions from others early on. Parent-teacher nights always surprised me. Parents always have questions, but with Jeremy on the roster, I had gotten several concerned inquiries. One parent said she was leaving my class immediately to go down to the principal to "get my son out of this classroom because Jeremy Johnson is in it!"

The tipping point came at the end of the following day. Delores said, "I cannot believe how much Jeremy likes you. Even though he has had male teachers before, he has never really connected with any of them like he has been connecting with you."

I like to be in control. And now I was very puzzled, feeling lots of insecurities, low, and extra defensive. Then I realized that her comment about Jeremy lifted me up. I couldn't help thinking of it all evening long, so the very next morning I began to wonder how I could help Delores feel as good as she made me feel the previous day. I asked her if she would like to take a more active role in our classroom. She eagerly accepted my invitation.

I explained that I had planned to split the students into small groups to debate an issue. I often used this teaching strategy as an informal assessment of how well I had covered the material in the current unit, and while I certainly didn't need her to help, it couldn't hurt.

We split the class into equal groups and each of us took a group. Each team was to choose five speakers to represent their group in a debate of the issue at hand. Each of the groups was to prepare a solid argument favoring their side of the debate. The students chosen would have to be able to discuss and represent their team's decision. I was shocked to find out that Delores had chosen Jeremy as one of the speakers. Certainly her students would not have done so. During the debate, everyone was excited and engaged. Jeremy was in such a flow it seemed he could have been on the high school debate team. You know how kids seem to have a better sense of the dynamics of the class than the adults often do? Well, the kids seemed to know that this was big. Jeremy was the kid they had feared throughout their early grades. But there they were, cheering him, congratulating him and his team for their performance. Kids were slapping him on the back, and for the first time, he wasn't hauling off and punching them. This was one of the most moving moments I had experienced in teaching, perhaps ever.

After that experience, Delores and I were so pumped that we decided to meet after school every Tuesday to see how we could do this co-teaching thing together. We had immediately seen what was possible and felt safe to honestly share our views of general education, special education, the community and its expectations, and our teaching styles.

These informal conversations grew to become some pretty amazing co-teaching units. We talked about who we were as teachers, like who we are, what we do on weekends, and our pet peeves. We were certainly different in some important generational ways, like in our tastes in music, political views, and how we spent our leisure time. But we did share a very strong work ethic—we agreed on which of the brand-new teachers we had already guessed were slackers. We were able to find common ground on things like the high expectations we both set for our students. We were able to create this foundation by talking through our issues, which helped us deal with our differences.

As we ventured into co-teaching, we tried to capitalize on the fact that Delores was an auditory learner and I was a kinesthetic learner. We had observed the difficulty many of our kids were having getting to work after we assigned a task. Delores took the lead in providing instructions while I showed students what the action looked like. The need to repeat instructions had been increasing and was costing us valuable instructional time. It was such a simple strategy, but we saw results, and this strategy made us realize that we needed to be much more intentional in how we observed our students and how we used that information to inform our classroom decisions. Playing to our own strengths made it more comfortable for both of us.

Unbeknownst to one another until our conversations started, both of us had collected a fair amount of information on the students, such as interest inventories that weren't reflected on their state achievement tests. After pooling that information, we felt confident we had enough information to help us differentiate our instruction. We also collected some interesting data on our respective school cultural environments. We made a surprise discovery. I had experienced accolades for most of my work life, in my corporate work, and even in my brief teaching profession stint. On the other hand, in her twenty years as a special educator, Delores had never had a colleague or administrator commend her work, other than casual but condescending remarks about how patient she must be to teach special education. In one evaluation, she actually heard a principal ask her if she was trying for extra stars in her crown in heaven by working with "those kids." Her colleagues only occasionally praised her—usually for keeping her students quiet and out of the office.

I took the lead with our lesson planning for the next few units while Delores grew in content expertise and confidence, and I increasingly trusted her abilities with the large group. When she noticed there was a unit on the Cold War era in our social studies text, she volunteered to share. Ronald Reagan had been her hero back in college, and she had saved lots of artifacts from that era. She planned a five-day social studies unit focused on the early 1980s and featuring the Cold War and Reagan. She planned with the depth and passion I would have, and literally transformed the general education curriculum far beyond the textbook. While she lectured on the political science, history, and geography of that time, we were able to set up a number of independent and small-group activities for enrichment and to help our strugglers. I could go that extra mile with some creative supports because she was taking the lead on the required content. We were both amazed at how engaged the class became and how well they did on the assessments at the end of the week. Little had Delores dreamed that she would ever be able to actually implement a unit on her hero when she developed it back in her preservice days.

As a treat the next week, we showed the movie *Miracle on Ice*. This had been my first real sports memory, so my engagement increased along with the students. Again, we hit pay dirt. I contacted a state professional hockey team that held their camps close to our school. The team was excited to come to the school to talk to the students, and that idea grew. Eventually, we were able to put up a temporary ice rink in the back playground, and the professional team played our sixth graders in a reenactment of *Miracle on Ice*.

Delores quickly came to know my students so well she could always improve on my ideas. Sometimes we plan units together from the ground up. She might develop a skeleton, and together we will plug in our state standards. And we can do this in little over an hour per week after school. This process has emerged as we have worked together. It works for us; it even energizes us.

Our weekly planning started with special education, initially focusing our conversations on the IEP goals for Jeremy, and then moving to what the rest of the class would do. Quickly we moved our focus to the standards at hand and worked backward to differentiate lessons for all of the students, thereby ensuring that not only Jeremy, but everyone in the class would benefit from more appropriate instructional matches. I might take the lead planning a language arts unit while Delores would chime in with an idea to illustrate a science aspect from the story with an experiment, sure that students like Morgan and Jessica would love that because they are more active learners. Eventually we were introduced to universal design for learning, and we eagerly considered several potential learning barriers and put their solutions into place, benefiting all of the students.

As far as designing and implementing co-teaching models, we just do it all together. It seems far less important to us to spend time on formula models than it does to plan our instruction. We figure out how to differentiate, formulate appropriate groupings, and then the teaching seems to take care of itself. If I had to name it, I would say generally we are teaming. Sometimes I will look to her and say, "This is what I am thinking about for the next unit. What do you think?" She serves as a filter, determining how to make it more successful for all of the kids.

During our second year co-teaching, we have been using the principles of UDL as we design our curriculum. We no longer retrofit our classroom for the challenges students might bring into our class. Using creative co-teaching roles, we feel we can know our students better by using a variety of preassessments. This allows us to provide them multiple pathways and reduce barriers, especially in the areas of representation, engagement, and expression. We feel that by differentiating the "what" of learning—academic content—and the "how" of learning—learning tasks—our students naturally stay engaged in the "why" of learning.

> There was a miracle in our sixth-grade *classroom*, too. As good as I thought I was, as hard as I worked, alone I could never have reached our kids better than I did when I co-taught with Delores. I don't mean to say that co-teaching has fixed everything. But our partnership helped improve Jeremy's productivity tenfold, and his social interaction even more. We all learned that he could be successful academically.

There are some additional highlights worth noting from this team that we can add to Taylor's story. The respect of students and adults is clearly one of the huge contributors to their success. The EL teacher who also worked with Taylor and Delores stated near the end of the school year that while she had been teaching for twenty-three years, she had always felt her colleagues never considered her a "real" teacher. In this school culture, she finally knew that she was considered a full member of the teaching profession.

Taylor and Delores have continued co-teaching and are sharing the wealth by splitting up their partnership, each taking new colleagues in various areas. The one thing they have insisted on is that the new partnerships begin by having conversations to find common ground and set high expectations for all students. They have developed a better communication plan for the open house at the beginning of the school year, and they are working together with the administrator to implement a professional learning community process with other teachers interested in improving their teaching practices through collaborative learning. This plan will allow them to videorecord their co-taught lessons and share them with other pairs of co-teachers or trusted colleagues for targeted professional development within the school.

Taylor's experience with Jeremy and Delores convinced him that there are many more students who can be taught in general education. These outliers are students, and they can meet high expectations—given the right situation and the right teachers.

By the end of the school year, the students and their parents were unanimous in looking at the class as a success story. The kids helped turn it around. Jeremy didn't just improve in the classroom, but he became a great offensive lineman. While football was so important in the community, it was also important for Jeremy to do well in his studies so he could remain eligible to play. It was a feather in many of the kids' caps that they began to embrace. Instead of having the community dread being around him, the kids saw that he could bring value and worth, and if they helped in the process, it would bring value and worth to them as well. The students became more perceptive of everyone's differences and were more intentional to include others.

We'll end this story with some words from Taylor:

> On the last day of school, Delores walked quietly into my room after the dismissal bell rung. She told me that most of our sixth graders had stopped by to thank her for helping them to learn. As she recounted that experience with "our kids," she was crying tears of joy. That was a beautiful moment in teaching.

Retooling Roles, Re-Assigning Resources

Like one of the universal design for learning schools we featured in chapter 1, Midfield High School received a PATINS technology grant. Midfield planned to provide change initiatives in assistive technology systems that impacted students in core curricular areas. The plan called for teachers to design lessons or units utilizing UDL strategies such as multiple means of representation, action and expression, and engagement in creating learning opportunities for diverse student populations. State test scores had been declining, and a growing community constituency was demanding more accountability. The social studies department was charged to lead the way for the whole district because of the strong and creative teachers on their team.

All five social studies department members were strongly grounded in and passionate about their content. They had the lowest number of discipline referrals of all departments based on a recent schoolwide positive behavior supports survey, and they genuinely liked collaborating together.

However, this story is unique in that the most difficult challenge was not raising students' low achievement scores. Rather, the department members found themselves regrouping to make accommodations for a special educator who was known to resist co-teaching and who had pushed to organize parents to petition that their students remain in her resource room.

Maria, a special educator, was assigned to teach a resource room one period a day and be with Dave for two periods of U.S. history and in geography for two periods with Kendall. Even though she had this arrangement for a couple of years, no one in the department could recall a time when she initiated an instructional strategy or modification or shared in the instruction. And even worse, she was notorious for making inappropriate statements and holding low expectations for her students. She became all the more vocal the previous year when her social studies resource students were reassigned from their resource room placements to general education core content classes, including enrollment in social studies classes with the existing team of teachers. Clearly this was an administrative problem, but for the time being, and despite numerous complaints, the situation did not improve.

Maria, the social studies teachers, and Larry, a technology educator, made up the PATINS team. They were given a few days of release time from teaching duties to collaboratively develop five UDL American history units in the state standards and content of American history that engage students' varying abilities.

Initially, the team's co-teaching conversations had been more narrowly focused on things like scheduling, getting extra teachers' manuals, sending out communication using all of the teachers' names, and grading. Unfortunately, the social studies teachers had not taken into account that the new members of their team might not share the same work ethic, expectations, content expertise, or commitment to teaching all students.

Maria had said very little during the initial planning sessions, but they attributed that to polite deference to their content expertise. And they also felt it was not unusual that Maria had not offered more specific ways that she might actually assist in the classroom because, after all, none of them had actually co-taught before. The book they all referred to suggested different models that seemed easy enough to incorporate into the daily lessons, but it had become clear to them that Maria did not have enough content knowledge to present new material, and she seemed intimidated to help students who were not on her students of record listing.

The first few weeks of school had become so stressful for Dave and Kendall that a special team meeting was called. They were feeling resentful of Maria for not pulling her weight. She was too timid to say anything in class, not to mention to co-teach. She deferred to them any time a student asked a question and basically milled around reminding students to sit up straight in their chairs. At the meeting, the team used a conversation prompt to help assess their strengths and challenges.

Because Maria was fearful she might lose her job with the next round of cutbacks due to tough economic realities in their district, she decided to cooperate. She admitted that she felt very intimidated by the content even though she had been responsible for teaching social studies in the resource room for a few years. This experience was now causing her to wonder if she had watered her curriculum down too much. She also confessed that she was intimidated getting up in front of a huge class; her comfort level was in small groups or individual work. And most of all she felt underqualified to be in the company of such a dynamic and talented group of colleagues. The more she confessed, the more overwhelmed she became, even offering to consider early retirement at the end of the semester. Dave and Kendall might have jumped to second that suggestion, but Larry reminded everyone that this was a collaborative process. Just because they had a rough start, they were all smart folks and could surely solve problems together to come up with a more positive solution. They took an informal team assessment and agreed on what they had going for them: interpersonal communication skills; a solid plan; time, energy, and expertise; passion for their content; and a commitment to serving their students.

In the end, they reconfigured Maria's role. She became the social studies learning consultant, working individually with all of the social studies teachers to proactively eliminate learning barriers using the UDL framework by providing more appropriate learning strategies for struggling students. In addition, the team redesigned the old resource room into a social studies resource center (SSRC) filled with iPod docking stations and other technology from the grant. Larry provided technical assistance to the teachers as well as the students. Larry and Maria were often called into classrooms by all of the teachers to help facilitate specific learning activities with small, targeted groups of students.

As the group examined their student data, they were able to come up with a plan they believed would increase learning and engagement for all students. The tipping point in their discussion came when they remembered that they shared the same goals for their students. Dave reminded them, "If we have different goals, our kids will be short-changed forever."

Universal design for learning units were designed to create engaging learning environments for all students. Supported by improved technology and using co-teaching strategies, the team declared their planning process to be a success. In order to balance out the classes fairly, students from the resource room were assigned to four of the five history classes. Kendall taught three of the classes, and Dave taught the other two. The group had planned for Maria to co-teach with Dave for two periods and with Kendall for two periods daily.

In no time, the SSRC became a popular place for students to gather to work on special projects and to research and collaborate with their team members. The special education room and its teacher lost their negative stigma, and it became a place where students could find additional supports. The plan became a success because the team differentiated, moving from a co-teaching to a consultation model of service delivery. In the end, Maria ended up with a much deeper understanding of history content, raised expectations for all of the students, and experienced a quality professional development opportunity each and every day. More importantly, she and her colleagues came to appreciate the unique contributions they could all make.

Once the team had decided to create the SSRC, they were intentional in getting the word out to all students and faculty about their newly created, universally designed SSRC and how it was supporting all students. While the team did not feel they could credit the resource center with improvements in test scores, they were able to track evidence in order to prove benefits to students in a variety of ways, beginning with student satisfaction surveys, increased rates of homework turned in, higher quality projects, and more effective collaborations and teaming. The team felt that for the first time, all of the students were included and supported in healthy ways, and stigmas had disappeared.

Controlled Chaos at the Human Circus

This fourth illustration tells the story of a dream come true. Many of us have probably wondered what it would be like to design our own school. The staff at Wiley School was able to do just that. People call Wiley a happy school all about sharing practice, learning through project-based problem solving, grouping, looping, and multiaging. You seldom see a teacher instructing independently. Collaboration permeates the philosophy and culture of this urban school. In Wiley's existence, teachers have demonstrated their exemplary work with student achievement test scores higher than the state average. Wiley has a huge community of admirers.

A participatory process at the beginning of each school year allows the entire faculty at Wiley to recommit to their original vision and set ambitious schoolwide goals for the coming year. Julie and Mark use the same process for their individual fifth-grade classes they are assigned as teachers for the year and then with their co-taught students during the first week of school. The group spends the first day re-establishing their relationships, working through protocols to catch up on one another's lives. They deal with their own assumptions and expectations for students, and use a variety of surveys and other instruments to orient new staff and to reacquaint each other in areas of strengths, uniqueness, specific skills, talents, learning and work preferences, aptitudes, pet peeves, and struggles. Teachers always report that this process has a way of fortifying and energizing them for the coming year, in part because of the reflections and reminders of why they had become educators in the first place.

Collaboration and co-teaching are so embedded in their daily policies, practices, and pedagogy that it is sometimes difficult to isolate the practice, even for the purpose of illustration. There are no pre-set "teaching teams," as the adults in the school rely heavily on student voice to follow passions, set learning goals, and guide the project-based problem-solving processes. This information and goal setting determine which team members can best meet the learning needs of the students. Thus, one of the most important teacher tasks at Wiley is to assemble the very best team for each unit so that the process is organic. The policies and procedures at the school accommodate this continual flux in teaching teams with flexibility and safe risk taking by making it possible to stretch across grade or content boundaries in assigning various teachers to teaching teams based on passions, goals, and the projects in progress.

Teachers sign up to engage in projects at Wiley, and many partners become integral to the instructional planning and teaching of unit lessons. Because of this, some observers might discount Wiley as an example of co-teaching, but we do not. Teachers don't just use their partners as guest speakers. They are extremely careful not to waste valuable instructional time with material that does not match or enhance the high learning outcomes they desire for their students. They also feel that a part of their mission is to inform the community of the rigors and authenticity of their instruction, while at the same time giving their teaching partners space and time to become even more informed about the needs and the potential challenges they face as teachers teaming with each other and with the students. All teachers continue to stretch themselves as they enlarge their teaching cadre with each new project.

During three days in late summer, Julie and Mark met to analyze and disaggregate the student data from the past spring, complete student rosters, schedule their classes, and begin designing their lessons and units of study. Every year, they developed a personalized learning plan (PLP) for all of the fifth graders. The plan included not only the state test scores, but also key data from the previous year's files. In addition, they included other preassessment tools, such as student and family surveys to help determine individual student interests, abilities, and learning preferences. In so doing, they let the information about their students drive their plans and how they scheduled the students throughout the day. In each of these iterations, the teachers discussed how they might use outside partners to meet their collective goals and to improve instruction for students.

The teachers have always approached their designs for instruction in creative and inclusive ways, and they are very experienced with using problem-based learning pedagogy. Julie and Mark delight in matching their curriculum and instruction to the needs of their students. They are committed to setting up positive classroom environments by providing clear expectations and spending time teaching protocols. Proactive by nature, they attempt to set up as many success strategies as possible and remove as many universal barriers as possible before they even begin with their students. Their PLPs include a checklist of possible supports to address barriers, as shown in figure 4.1.

Figure 4.1: Problem-based learning plan checklist.

Student Struggles	Possible Personalized Learning Plan Strategies for Success
Cannot read at grade level	
Has difficulty comprehending the material	
Has difficulty mastering the vocabulary of the unit	
Has difficulty with handwriting (speed or accuracy)	
Has difficulty with calculating activities	
Needs help with conducting research	
Needs instructional material in a language other than English	
Needs additional challenges	
Does best individually/in small groups/in large groups	
Benefits from making modifications and accommodations	
Needs protocols and procedures to revisit	
Needs organizational skills to revisit	
Needs scaffolding	
Other	

*Visit **go.solution-tree.com/specialneeds** to download and print this figure.*

While this form is invaluable as Julie and Mark plan for the whole class, they also keep abbreviated checklists available for instructional aides, families, and the community volunteers who frequently visit their classroom.

A process of backward planning drives all curricular design and instruction decisions for the PLPs as they decide on key decision points for instructional design and delivery. Planning sessions always include such items as desired results, goals or standards, and decision points for what the team wants each of their students to know, understand, and be able to do.

Wiley's flexible scheduling also gives Julie and Mark the opportunity to be creative with their colleagues from other grade levels. For example, before school starts, Julie and Mark will collaborate with the fourth- and sixth-grade teams to see how they all might create flexible groupings using the singular math curriculum and grouping students for the best possible instructional matches. A couple of the students might be better matched instructionally if placed with groupings in the fourth grade, while five students would be better served in sixth-grade groups. While this can be a coordination nightmare in the beginning, soon it is what Julie and Mark call "creative chaos at the human circus." It is manageable because the results help create a win-win for all.

Past fifth-grade teams have focused on a variety of community social justice issues the students have identified. For example, the *Helping the Homeless* project team included Julie, Mark, the English learning teacher, and the social worker. It also included two exceptional community partners with whom the students connected. Because of the structure of the class and the integral involvement of the community partners, the group of adults was able to implement a full-blown teaming effort throughout the unit. These outside partners helped expand student learning, and they themselves became educated about what quality learning looks like and expanded their views about using collaboration to strengthen learning.

The *Water, Water Everywhere and Nothing to Drink* project ended up being a two-part effort. For the first unit, the science teacher from the new technical high school around the corner was able to use his free periods to come to Wiley to co-teach science classes. Mark and Julie designed several learning stations. Some of those could be conducted in the science lab, but one was held at the local university science department in partnership with Richard, the head of their science department. Students learned some basics about pollution and water safety. Garcia, one of the sixth-grade teachers, helped Julie and Mark decide which science and math learning standards to focus on as they designed and implemented a number of learning stations both in the classroom and on the banks of the local creek that students had suspected of being polluted. Garcia was a long-standing member of several environmental groups in town.

It wasn't long before the second unit began to emerge. Garcia had whetted the appetites of the students to address a social justice issue. Troubled by the pollution they found, they were ready for action. The teachers added Garcia and Fred, the fine arts teacher, to help design and implement the second unit, this time addressing standards in language arts (especially writing and presentation skills) and social studies (roles and responsibilities of local, state, and national government). In the end, the students were able to make a strong case before their local partners group as practice before their meeting with the county commissioners and the city planning and zoning board. The standing ovations for their students assured Mark and Julie that the extra time and effort to develop co-teaching partnerships had paid off in ways they could never have imagined.

Julie and Mark and their Wiley colleagues are quite appreciative of the opportunities they have in learning to work together and to establish a learning environment that is conducive to the seamless, supportive, universally accessible philosophy they sought collectively.

Clearly an overriding factor in the success of this dream team school remains the passion that the adults and the students bring to the school and their increasing outreach to others who can help them co-teach even more effectively. While they don't have the challenging restrictions most of us find ourselves governed by, they do serve to expand our thinking about how and where we might find and enlist new co-teaching partners.

Carrie's Story

This story comes directly from one of us. Carrie had a chance to bring co-teaching to higher education. She was charged with helping develop a new preservice teaching curriculum. Her institution was awarded funding to train soon-to-be student teachers as well as their mentor teachers in co-teaching. Her example shows a very intentional plan the university faculty devised that used a change process to help the co-teaching program grow, expand, and sustain itself.

Roma ventured into co-teaching as an experienced second-grade cooperating teacher. She had supported preservice teachers in many capacities and enjoyed the opportunity of bringing young teachers into the profession. Uncertain how the co-teaching experience might unfold, yet always open to meaningful change, Roma climbed aboard the co-teaching bandwagon in January with the state university's teacher preparation program.

She welcomed Billie, an early childhood education major, into her second-grade classroom as a co-teaching partner. Billie had been assigned to make classroom observations and complete short-term field experiences in other settings prior to her student teaching, but opportunities to actually deliver lessons had been limited. A week before her co-teaching placement began, she admitted her ambivalence to her university supervisor by voicing such comments as, "I'm getting nervous, but I'm really excited to start!" Reassured that her nervousness was a good sign, she was encouraged by her supervisor's prediction that "It will all go well!"

Roma and Billie began their journey together on January 8 as they came together at a full-day training session and discussed everything from second-grade core content to traits about their own personalities. As a winter storm outside slowed campus and K–12 schools to a snail's pace, Roma and Billie moved from conversations about their relationship to dedicated planning with other co-teachers as they prepared for the adventure ahead. They started small, with focused conversations on their own teaching philosophies, ideas about how students learn, ideas on classroom management, and the logistics of setting up a classroom they shared.

Roma used the next few sessions to acquaint Billie with the students they would share, familiarizing her with the state standardized tests and other evidence she had collected during the fall semester that seemed relevant for their instructional decisions. The two of them also examined the curriculum for the semester in all content areas. It was a lot of information to digest, but Billie's previous work in the school in an earlier field experience had informed her of the district's basic elementary curriculum. They worked together on the curriculum mapping to pull out the most important focus areas in order to design lessons that would address the students' range of academic and social diversity.

After those initial training and planning days, they scheduled regular daily co-planning sessions when Roma shared an upcoming unit overview before they jointly decided on the standards and understandings they wanted for their students. They spent time designing the assessments they would use, both formative and summative. During January, Roma and Billie immersed themselves in their shared classroom. One of their first successful co-taught math lessons involved using manipulatives and interactive whiteboard technology. Using the side-by-side, alternative strategies, Roma observed:

> We could not have done this lesson without two teachers. Having one teacher use manipulatives to support a small group of students who needed review on the concept while the other teacher led the whole class with student volunteers on the SMART Board, that was the best way to address our diverse student needs.

Throughout the rest of the semester, they touched base about curriculum delivery and student needs. Before, during, and after school, whenever they could, they carved out the time because they saw the value of those conversations that included comments like:

> "Did you notice how they . . . ?"
> "Yes, and it made me think about the way we . . ."
> "Maybe we could try to . . ."
> "Could I share an idea like that that I was thinking of . . . ?"
> "Let's talk some more about how we could make that work . . ."

And so it went, for sixteen weeks—sharing roles, learning from each other, and making a difference. Using small groups to advance learning became a true "aha!" moment for both co-teachers. Billie began a reading intervention for her students that would soon result in significant improvement for her struggling students. Billie, Roma, and additional staff members were able to plan and differentiate instruction to meet the needs of all their students.

At the close of their experience, both teachers reflected on their co-teaching journey. Roma commented:

> I really see the importance of small groups to address the differences in our students' needs. Next year, I have to find a way to continue co-teaching, even without a student teacher. We already have a strong grade-level team, and it makes sense to add the EL teacher who already provides service to a good percentage of our students. Having her as an official team member will be my first step in making this go farther! It's so important to work together with others. This was fun! Billie has a true heart for the kids. She understands their differences. What she has done makes students look to her as a teacher.

And Billie added:

> Working in a classroom with high standards for all students is an inspiration. This is how it should be. It's all about the students. That's what we're here for. This is the one job I've really loved, and I wasn't even paid!

Billie learned about what it means to be a true professional as you continually attempt to find a better instructional match for all students. Being mentored closely by an experienced professional allowed her to move away from the often traditional student-teaching structure of "watch me this week—now they're yours." The experience launched her into the profession with a better appreciation for the power of collaboration, and she came to understand the importance of the up-front conversations that are necessary in order to establish initial roles and responsibilities for each of the partners who share practices.

Roma plans to share her collaborative experience with Billie to the rest of the faculty in hopes of recruiting other potential educators, and she can then enlarge the second-grade team by including the primary EL teacher.

"Just Do It!" Co-Teaching: What It's Not, and What It Can Be

Luke is an extraordinary English teacher and special educator who co-teaches in a large suburban high school. His partnerships have run the gamut from those of mild resistance to a partnership that has helped expand and improve all areas of his practice. Luke's commitment to quality teaching, his understanding of how people change, and his own willingness to differentiate strategies have helped him overcome challenges and experience a multitude of successes. Luke tells his story in his own words in the text that follows.

Co-teaching is more a frame of mind than it is a specific model or lesson plan. Licensed to teach both special education and English, I have been co-teaching at our high school with various colleagues for seven years now. In my preservice training, I was introduced to co-teaching, but it was never really modeled or encouraged. My special education classes mostly focused on the laws, disability categories, and the whole IEP case-conference process.

And yet I had never really wanted to teach in a resource room by myself. It never made sense to teach a room full of kids who had been identified as needing lots of support. It seemed to me those kinds of groupings usually came with lots of lowered expectations as well. Working with another professional colleague seemed a much better way to go; it is easier to find solutions to challenges. If you are having a bad day, your partner can pick up the slack. You have so many other options—the old "two brains, two approaches" mindset. I always felt one teacher was often just crop dusting, but having a partner allowed the pair to go deeper into practice, providing robust instruction for students.

Quite honestly, most general educators were glad to hear that I was going to come in and help. Having built up my reputation in the high school, they seemed to know that I would actively plan and teach, not just hang out with the IEP kids.

There were co-teaching challenges in our building that made others skeptical, usually stemming from special educators not showing up or coming in notoriously late to class. The opposite happened to me. One particular teacher hadn't wanted to partner, but when she saw the value of what I brought to her classes, she would walk out as I came in, feeling that my effort could free up time for her to do other things. The students seemed to like that model. They asked, "Hey, does she have to come back?"

Challenges usually stemmed from partners failing to agree on a commonly shared vision for teaching and learning. I'm fairly clear about my beliefs about that, so I would seek out partners with whom I could at least have the important conversations and come to some mutually acceptable plan of action. And even when that did occur, there were the subtle things that crept in from time to time that reminded you that sometimes what we say doesn't always align with what we do.

No doubt about it, the most important conversation is that critical conversation where you and your partner talk about who has responsibility for the students. Are they *your* students? Are they *my* students? Or are they *our* students? What is my responsibility? Do I serve all of the kids in the class, or just the ones on my roster? Having those conversations up front will make a real difference in how you proceed.

Before class ever started, I wanted my partners to know that I would be actively involved and wanted to get to know them. For most general educators, that was a refreshing thing to hear.

This relationship piece goes back to my own experiences in high school. The teachers I liked had all made a personal connection to me. They shared a part of their life with me: one went to Woodstock, one served in Vietnam. They were real people, and because they were willing to share some of themselves, they were more effective in teaching me.

When you have a shared vision, it will help you plan your approach and be more successful in your collaborations. The leadership in a school sends a really important message about how students are valued in a school. They set the tone for what kids we think can and can't be successful. If the prevailing thought in the building is that not all kids can learn, then developing a shared vision is much more difficult.

Creating a shared vision is more difficult than it might appear to be. One of my co-teachers sauntered down the hallway on numerous occasions, running his pencil down the class list.

"Hey, Luke, I believe this is one of yours," he would begin.

I would invariably respond, "Well, Joe, I believe he is one of yours, too. He has the same standards as the rest of your class."

Joe never changed, but he would happily tell you that he was in a great co-teaching arrangement with me.

Getting the pragmatics right can be challenging in co-teaching partnerships. What about space, communication, responsibilities, grading, parents, generational issues, and personal preferences? All partners are different, but for me, it has been important to have a desk, space, a place where I can bring in photos of my kids, cat, vacation with friends, things to make it lived in. This space, these artifacts, make a powerful statement that we share the room and the teaching and learning.

As for communication, we list both of our names on the door, on student handouts, and on all letters and notes home. We are equally accessible for parents. None of our families wanted noninclusive settings, and we attribute that in part to the fact that we were very clear from the beginning about our standards and that both of us were in the classroom as a way to support all students. If anything, there are higher standards. We all get better when we work together.

For many special educators, lack of content expertise can cause problems of trust and parity, making the assigning of roles and responsibilities look quite different. Our conversations on curriculum usually focused on grading, discipline, and spelling tests. Sometimes we would decide to delete a particular part of the curriculum and instead use primary and other resources. Other times we would teach fairly traditionally.

With effective partnerships, it doesn't matter who does the grading. For example, both of us would read and grade assigned student essays so we could both get a better picture of what was going on in class. We might discover that a problem was not just a special education issue, but it was troubling for all of the students. I'm not sure in a traditional setting that a general education teacher would do this.

What about parents? Parents are just interested in knowing you are there to help their kids be successful, even if you are the special educator. Generational issues can be a big deal, though. For example, I taught with a terrific teacher—number of years in the building, great reputation. He went berserk when kids said "suck." In my book, this wasn't such a big deal. We had to talk about whether it was cause for a trip to the principal's office.

Personal preferences are another challenging issue. Do we agree that all materials should look professional? Is there a quality check? I taught with a very capable partner; we got along great, but she had this quirky habit of using cutesy fonts on all of the student handouts. Not something I couldn't adjust to, except that many of the "little kid" fonts had the s and r characters backwards—cute, but totally inappropriate for students with dyslexia or other learning challenges. And yes, there was the lady who loved the scented candles. Caused my allergies to go bonkers! We needed to talk.

We usually had little time, so we tried to move quickly into discussions about what our students should know and be able to do. We tried to answer questions such as these: What are the activities that will help students be successful? What are the evidence-based practices we should be considering? I always try to leave planning meetings armed with an instructional design and implementation for the unit ahead and know who is responsible for materials, who would deliver what parts, and so on.

We started with the general education standards and tried to make changes to meet the IEP requirements, mostly by improvising the planning, not so much in terms of differentiating our instruction or the tasks we were asking our students to perform. We would co-present, and then we might drop into other co-teaching strategies like setting up learning centers or multiple flexible groupings. It really came down to using strategies that just made sense. We designed and taught good lessons, almost always based on a thorough preassessment instrument, such as a readiness checklist, or guided questions, or exit questions from a previous class session.

Most of my partners preferred having a scheduled planning time after school, and my time with each of them was different. Often it meant that I would have to plan twice or three times, depending on how many teachers I shared classes with, and they understood that.

One year I remember I was scheduled to co-teach with three different English teachers. All of us had some experience with the others in the group, and we all were assigned to teach other sections of English classes that were not co-taught, referred to at our school as the noninclusion classes. (At our high school, co-teaching is *code* for inclusion.) So the three of us set up joint planning time. We met once a week to plan for our two classes each that we shared, and those plans would invariably spill over into the noninclusion classes. Those planning sessions proved invaluable to me as a constant check of what was important in the curriculum. Quite honestly, I felt that the students in our resource rooms were often getting cheated out of quality curricular lessons.

Typically, my partners and I would prepare lesson plans or units that provided different roles for each of us, and every week I would take responsibility to prepare certain materials, lessons, or presentations. They knew the work was going to get done for kids and there would be two of us to share in it. Planning sessions ran the gamut, again depending on the relationship, the students, and our desired learning outcomes. With the more casual partners, the conversation would usually focus on strategies that do not require a lot of time and energy.

For the past three years, my partner and I have reserved every Thursday night to meet at a favorite local spot, grab dinner and a drink, and do our planning for the coming week. We often compare the stacks of themes we just graded using a rubric we created. This gives both my partner and me a much better idea of how all of our students are doing and helps inform our planning in a way I can't imagine doing without.

For our efforts, we see outcomes such as these: we get a better sense of our kids, we are able to keep them more engaged in authentic learning, and our overall classroom passing rates have improved. I was able to build better relationships within the department, which led to better communication between the English department colleagues and with the special education department, so everybody wins!

What made the really good partnerships work was that we knew one another, so we didn't have to play games. We approached this partnership as true professionals. Good general educators plan appropriately for all students, and good special educators never sit back and watch their partners work.

When you gain administrative support, you can earn some flexibility and choice. We learned from one another. For example, on the last day of class, the students filled out a course evaluation. So we got feedback on how to improve for the coming year. We also go to conferences together, whether it is for special education or English, because we know we both have more skills to learn, and learning together is more fun.

As I reflect on my co-teaching experiences, I do wonder about other methods of teaching. Pete and I would like nothing better than teaching together until we both retire to our fishing boats, but I wonder, should we be sharing the wealth? Could we both move to other teaching partnerships and share what we have learned, help stretch other professionals, benefit more students?

Summary: Sharing the Success

All of these stories share common co-teaching themes that illustrate some of the developmental aspects of collaboration and highlight experiences teachers have along the way. The framework offers you and your partner a way to develop common understandings, investigate your own assumptions and practices in pursuit of instructional improvement, and design and implement an enhanced shared practice. Whether you are just beginning or have been long-time collaborators, we invite you to talk.

Collaborative efforts are increasing as more schools begin to move from inclusion that looks only at the academic, physical, and social aspects of a school to a more multilevel system of support. Most of the partners we have featured in this chapter began their journeys with a desire to work with a partner or team in order to be more inclusive. We have watched them grow to embrace a more universally designed environment, raising expectations and minimizing deficit-based mindsets. These educators are working together to design environments that eliminate as many barriers to success as possible and add creative and meaningful supports for all students.

When the collaborative process works, there is always a relentless commitment to engage more students more effectively in the classroom. Effective classrooms come when we provide quality instruction, whether solo, through co-teaching with one partner, or when teaching with an entire team. In the end, almost all of the co-teachers we have ever worked with say that if they had their choice, they wouldn't do it any other way.

There are rare partnerships that meet and seem to click from their first introductions. Other teams struggle and never seem to get in sync. We know that if you and your partners approach the conversation process as professionals with open minds and a willingness to use this as a quality professional development opportunity, you will find your own timing, and it will be just the amount that you need. Trust the process, and have fun as you learn about yourselves and your work together. Then, as you grow and develop as a co-teaching partnership, consider the next steps of how to expand and sustain your efforts on a wider basis. Chapter 5 provides a further step in using conversations and protocols or activities to extend your base of support systemwide for the continued progress of quality co-teaching partnerships.

5

EXPANDING CO-TEACHING CONVERSATIONS

> ### Conversation Starters
>
> - How do we create a professional development plan to ensure growth and sustainability for our collaborative and co-teaching efforts?
> - What is our communications plan to ensure that all administrators and stakeholders are informed and engaged in our collaborative efforts?
> - How will we pursue generative possibilities to build and sustain individual and organizational capacity?
> - How can we recognize and acknowledge our successful collaborative efforts?

As we learned in chapter 4, the keys to beginning a quality co-teaching practice include participating in value-added conversations that engage our co-teaching partners, examining student data, and working to enhance instruction. Once these value-added conversations have been entered into and established, many co-teachers and administrators wonder if they are capable of spreading the wealth to other colleagues in a more systemic approach to implementation of co-teaching. This chapter will guide you toward this larger goal. The conversation starters at the beginning of this chapter provide a focal point for this process. The rationale and important definitions within this process are highlighted in the text that follows.

Rationale and Definitions

Embarking on any new instructional approach requires some degree of change within a school or district. For co-teaching partners who are committed to expanding that change beyond their own classrooms, various attitudes, knowledge, and skills are required to move individual conviction and commitment forward with colleagues (Tan & Kaufmann, n.d.). Becoming agents of change in a school or organization requires a clear understanding and consideration of how other individuals may be impacted by the change. Specific concerns include the motivation of others and the need for increased knowledge as it relates to the detailed points of co-teaching (Hutton, n.d.; Rea & Connell, 2005b). DuFour and Eaker (1998) caution all change agents and organizations working through a change process to be mindful of the common mistakes made during any change, including these mistakes most relevant for our purposes: permitting structural and cultural obstacles to block the change process and undercommunicating the vision. These common errors in judgment affect quality change and speak strongly to the need for plans that will guide the future direction and learning of the faculty. And, as Scruggs, Mastropieri, and McDuffie (2007) found through a metasynthesis of qualitative co-teaching research, administrative support and teacher training are needed to reap the most benefits from changing to a co-teaching model of instruction.

A quality *professional development plan* is an important component in any school or districtwide approach. This is one of the only ways in which co-teaching can grow outside the walls of single classrooms. Teachers and administrators need to purposefully plan professional development experiences that ensure continued growth and development of collaborative practice and co-teaching. It is especially important to keep in mind a learning-oriented model that supports adult development (Drago-Severson, 2004, 2008). The three most common adult ways of knowing are (1) instrumental—having a very concrete orientation to life, (2) socializing—thinking abstractly but subordinating one's own ways of knowing to the opinions of others, and (3) self-authoring—generating one's own internal value system with ownership and responsibility. These adult ways of knowing can be accommodated through professional development that recognizes teaming and provides leadership roles, collegial inquiry, and mentoring (Drago-Severson, 2008). This type of a professional development plan might include: external consultants, training workshops, in-school observations and coaching, school-site visits, peer networks, and learning community study groups. All of these options should be implemented to provide a variety of experiences for teachers that move them outside their own classrooms with time to rethink practice and perspective (Fullan, 2001; McLaughlin & Talbert, 2006). Peer coaching among and between co-teaching partners may provide another method to accomplish adult-centered learning (Buzbee Little, 2005). Various modes of professional development will be needed, depending on individual teachers, co-teaching partners, and school structure.

Ongoing professional development will also be an important consideration to allow co-teaching partnerships to continue to learn and grow together. Adequate time for learning, practice, and reflection can also provide avenues for that growth. Part of this type of professional development may include facilitating co-teachers to become instructional leaders (Lambert, 1998). Teacher leaders who gain skill and understanding in adult development, dialogue, collaboration, and organizational change can be great assets to personal and schoolwide professional development plans that augment the co-teaching instructional practices.

A *communications plan* serves as a guide or template for who, what, and when information about your co-teaching partnership should be shared. Various people inside and outside of the school system must understand the purpose and your beliefs in that purpose to be able to put their own support behind your efforts (McLaughlin & Talbert, 2006). Building, district, or system administrators, teachers' organizations, professional developers, parents, and community members may all be stakeholders in your efforts. Co-teaching goals, objectives, audiences, tools, timelines, and evaluations will be important to consider in communicating the crucial aspects of your work to others. This can include all oral, written, and electronic forms of communication utilizing a variety of media sources. Being sure that all of the various stakeholders are aware of the co-teaching quality, results, and progress of your initiative is central to your efforts to expand the impact beyond just a single partnership (Hirsh, 2008; Sparks, 2007).

Capacity of both individuals and the organization (school or district) is critical to consider in moving co-teaching into a more systemwide teaching approach for adding instructional value. Fullan's (2006) definition for capacity building fits well for our purposes here:

> A policy, strategy, or action taken that increases the collective efficacy of a group to improve student learning through new knowledge, enhanced resources, and greater motivation on the part of people working individually and together. (p. 60)

Thus, an intentionally planned strategy or action will have to be developed in order to achieve real capacity building in regard to expanding the co-teaching practice. General issues of how co-teaching fits into schools can also be categorized as issues and strategies related to content, structure, assessment, and diversity (Dieker & Murawski, 2003). Taking these general issues and strategies and itemizing them into smaller, more discrete areas of focus and work will help the key players address each detail that affects capacity. Factors to consider for how more teachers and schools can be brought on board and prepared to implement the various co-teaching models include number of students and classrooms, number of teachers, knowledge and experience level of teachers and administrators, levels of support, and so on.

This process is intended to be *generative* (developmental and creative) in its essence and will facilitate people having enough time and space to work toward developing co-teaching capacity. The complexity of building capacity in the multilayer systems of schools requires a concentrated effort with no prepackaged or "one size fits all" solutions (Kahane, 2007).

Tracking the goals and progress of any co-teaching instructional implementation requires the development of an *accountability plan*. The rationale and development of such a plan for co-teaching should be similar to following the progress of any other instructional models used where internal accountability should precede external accountability (Elmore, 2004). Teachers and administrators should always ask:

- What do we want our students to know and be able to do?
- How will we know whether our students are achieving or attaining the goals and standards we have set?
- How will we gather and monitor the necessary student performance information?
- How will we set and measure progress toward our school goals?
- How will we use the student and school performance information we have gathered?
- How will we communicate our plan and the results?
- Are there additional organizational structures or policies that need to be developed and implemented to support this instructional model?
- What successes will we celebrate? How will we celebrate the successes of our students and our co-teaching partnerships?

Consideration of the meaningful roles of each teacher in the classroom, the strategies teachers use to promote success for all students, the evidence of that success through accurate data on co-teaching, and what the impact may be for furthering the practice beyond individual partnerships are necessary to continue to move forward with a workable accountability plan (Wilson, 2005).

The last questions noted above, "What successes will we celebrate? How will we celebrate the successes of our students and our co-teaching partnerships?," focus us on the importance of real recognition and *celebration of accomplishment* with the new co-teaching instructional model and the change occurring within classrooms and schools. This recognition is a crucial step in the life cycle of collaboration and leadership within schools (Rubin, 2007). Celebration provides a welcome bridge between implementation, assessment and evaluation, and adjusted implementation. Thus the natural progression from being successful implementers of new co-teaching instructional models can then be followed by a desire and impetus to be change initiators within a larger context of the wider school or district organization. The conversations can support this movement forward in a broader context within your schools.

Roma and Billie: Expanding Their Impact

As Roma and her student teacher, Billie, were winding down their spring semester co-teaching partnership, they began to plan what should come next in the near future. Each co-teacher was committed to continuing her own professional growth and development, and also to being an advocate for co-teaching and collaborative practices within her school (or future school).

All of Roma's second-grade teaching colleagues had been interested in hearing updates about her co-teaching student-teaching situation throughout the spring, so Roma decided to share even more information with them. The primary EL teacher already served quite a few of Roma's second graders through pull-out services and consultation to the second-grade team. She became a natural fit to be involved in any future information sharing. Roma proposed that they investigate ways they could all support their diverse group of students even more inclusively. At their end-of-school team meeting, she shared the statement from the National Staff Development Council (NSDC, now Learning Forward) on professional development with its emphasis on being comprehensive, sustained, intensive, and every day. Roma also explained the steps needed to ensure that their own professional development exemplified teaching effectiveness focused on raising student achievement (NSDC, n.d.).

Billie was completing her degree and starting the job-search process, but she definitely knew she wanted to continue with professional development opportunities in co-teaching and the quality mentoring that had been such an important part of her own student-teaching experience. As she prepared her resume, she made sure to emphasize the professional development and experiences she gained in her time in Roma's classroom.

Along with these teachers, the professors and staff at her university's teacher education program continued to plan learning and training opportunities for its Professional Development School (PDS) partners. A global plan emerged using the student-teaching/co-teaching semester as the end outcome, with a gradual "backwards movement" into each prior semester in the program. Learning Forward professional development precepts were used as guides in planning meetings with each PDS, university faculty, and other university staff who would be part of the training implementations across the curriculum (NSDC, n.d.).

The university faculty and staff directly responsible for the coordination of the student-teaching semester realized how important a communication plan would be to the continuation of these co-teaching efforts. Throughout that first spring semester of implementation, three faculty members met with each PDS administrative team and shared the research and contextual background on co-teaching both generally and specific to the designed plan. University supervisors who were directly responsible for the co-teaching teams in each district were instrumental in providing "on the ground" data and stories of how each co-teaching relationship was progressing along with K–12 student responses to the new model of student teaching. Additionally, the university personnel shared much of the general data on co-teaching and the specifics of the student-teaching focus with other university faculty who had direct responsibility for preparing preteachers in education or academic content methods courses in earlier semesters. It was vitally important to keep the administrative teams and other university faculty updated on each major aspect of the program's progression and the impact on their preteachers, teachers, and students.

Co-teaching teams of cooperating teachers and student teachers gathered bimonthly for additional content training in various aspects of co-teaching and mentoring. At each of these gatherings, university faculty and staff gathered additional input and feedback from the teams to help fine tune or adjust materials, resources, and evaluation instruments. An article was published in the university's PDS magazine focusing on this new student-teaching approach of co-teaching. This same information was then used by each PDS in their newsletters or district-based memos to share the involvement of schools and teachers in this new venture with the university. Thus the program was communicated within and beyond the boundaries of the PDS organizational structure. Cooperating teachers and their principals also used this vehicle to share with those teachers not currently a part of the co-teaching program with an eye on expanding the knowledge and interest in their own future participation. At the university level, the same was happening between current faculty participants and their colleagues who were needed to expand the co-teaching emphasis into other coursework.

Roma, the cooperating teacher, had begun her own proactive steps for helping the co-teaching model grow among other colleagues at her school. She openly shared at both grade-level meetings and full-faculty meetings what she and her co-teaching partner, Billie, the university student teacher, were learning in their workshops. A fourth-grade teacher in the building, Sharon, was also involved in the co-teaching project with her student teacher, Whitney. The two partnerships began meeting every other week to share ideas or questions that had arisen during their planning or teaching time together. This foursome became quite a partnership of power in explaining new resources they had gathered from their university supervisor or in the additional bimonthly training sessions the university hosted for all of the co-teaching partners.

As the university co-teaching program faculty and staff worked during the spring semester in the teaching-team trainings, they knew they had to also liaison with each of the PDS districts in ways that went further than just a focus on the current cooperating teachers within each school. Working closely with the administrative teams and their respective university supervisors, focus groups were interviewed in each district to ascertain the content information needs, interest levels, and mentor qualities of other teachers who would be the next co-teaching partners for the fall-semester student teachers. Onsite trainings were planned and readied for implementation in the summer so that all new co-teaching partnerships would be ready to start the fall semester feeling confident in their knowledge, skills, and beliefs about their joint teaching practice.

Some PDS sites requested additional co-teaching and mentoring training from the university team as part of their school improvement plan. Two schools that were researching options for working more collaboratively as a K–12 faculty while meeting the needs of their increasingly diverse student body studied the university presentation materials that the administrative team in their district shared with them. These schools made joint decisions that utilizing a co-teaching model would be the best way to take full advantage of the assets their special educators and EL teachers offered to all teachers and students. In the summer, additional co-teaching and mentoring training was scheduled for these school faculties. Since the majority of teachers in these buildings had already received much of the co-teaching training from the university, it was a natural transition to look at these sites as the next quality locations to embed future student teachers in the co-teaching model. Building the capacities of individual school sites to work in collaborative teaching teams greatly increased the university's ability to place additional student teachers in already-prepared schools.

In the day-to-day schedules of teaching, it is often easy to forget the importance of taking time for acknowledging and celebrating successes. The university, PDS districts, schools, and teachers specifically planned together for the various ways each of them should also focus on positive outcomes and progress in their co-teaching work. Co-teaching partners Roma and Billie, along with Sharon and Whitney, had been collecting data on their students' assignment completion, daily grades, and behavior referrals. These data points were the same ones their school had focused on in the previous fall semester as part of the schoolwide plan for classroom improvement. In each case, the data during the spring co-teaching semester showed gradual improvement. Additionally, each co-teaching partnership developed a short survey to gather information about student opinions regarding this new model of teaching and teacher support.

These two partner teams developed ways to celebrate their gains in completing homework, daily grade improvement, and the decrease in behavior referrals seen both in the playground and in school settings. Just as important as celebrating with their classrooms, the adults also planned for team celebrations to acknowledge their positive work together—before- or after-school breaks at the local coffee shop, simple and inexpensive gifts that were used in the classroom, or celebration signs that they posted on their desks or computers as reminders of how worthwhile their co-teaching endeavor was in the classroom. The school also found ways to affirm the co-teaching work and the partnership with the university student-teaching program. A weekly schoolwide memo always had a short news item on co-teaching, and the monthly faculty meetings typically included some sharing time from all grade levels on their progress toward the schoolwide classroom improvement goals. Celebrations were thus shared horizontally and vertically throughout the schools during this first semester of implementing the co-teaching model.

Celebrating the PDS partnerships and the co-teaching implementation in each district was also a major focus of the university. The faculty and staff responsible for the liaison work between each district and the coordination of the co-teaching program hosted a celebratory event during each semester of the academic year. PDS administrative teams, university supervisors, and various other K–12 and university faculty involved in the co-teaching process were guests at the festivities. Attendees shared public acknowledgments and small token gifts of appreciation. The story of co-teaching and its impact on K–12 student learning and student teacher achievements was a highlight of the celebration. Future steps in the university-PDS partnerships were stressed as a positive end to the event.

Roma and Billie's story continues as more schools are brought into PDS status and ever-increasing numbers of administrators, teachers, and student teachers become partners in the co-teaching program. This story featured examples from the non-negotiable conversations protocols for expanding impact. As you grow your capacity and want to move your co-teaching partnerships and support even further, be sure to tap into the deeper conversations in the special occasion and in a perfect world protocols. They will serve to elevate your work even further.

Summary: Creating a School Culture

This final set of conversations in the value-added co-teaching framework has brought more teachers and administrators to an explicit understanding of all that is involved in moving individual co-teacher practices into the mainstream of a school or district culture. Using the conversation protocols related to professional development, communication building, sustaining capacity, and celebration will expand your co-teaching impact within the larger school community.

CRITICAL CONVERSATIONS PROTOCOLS: SET 1— ENGAGE PARTNERS

This chapter is the first of four chapters that contain the detailed conversations protocols or plans that will help you and your partner or team develop more effective co-teaching practice. In this chapter, you will find the critical conversations protocols for set 1, Engage Partners. The chapter begins with focus questions and anticipated outcomes and contains three types of conversations: (1) non-negotiable, (2) special occasion, and (3) in a perfect world.

The focus questions will give you an idea of what you'll learn in this set of protocols. The outcomes provide measures to help you determine if you and your partner have covered the kinds of conversations that will help you be successful when you move to the next set. The Reflective Journal (page 46) will help you monitor your progress through the series of protocols.

Visit **go.solution-tree.com/specialneeds** to download the reproducibles for this chapter.

Focus Questions

- What do we need to talk about to develop our professional relationship?
- How can we create a shared vision for all students?
- How can we address the practicalities of our partnership?
- How can we develop agreement on the roles and responsibilities for our partnership?

Anticipated Outcomes

- We have begun conversations to develop our collaborative professional relationship.
- We have developed a shared vision for all of our students.
- We have developed agreements on the practicalities of our partnership.
- We have developed an agreement on the roles and responsibilities for our partnership.

NON-NEGOTIABLE CONVERSATIONS

Building a Relationship — *Relationship-Building Protocol*

Establishing a collaborative relationship is perhaps the most important aspect of the collaborative process. It won't really matter how you organize your joint space, examine the data, or implement co-teaching models unless you and your partner are well acquainted and come to some common understandings about who you are as partners. The more time you are able to spend establishing a positive collaborative relationship, the more success and enjoyment you will have. Partners who take the necessary time to do this can experience an interdependent relationship wherein they complement one another and add value to their teaching through their collaborative efforts. True collaborative partners share a vision, beliefs, and values, and they use norms to guide their work. They share a mutual commitment to improve student learning for all students.

As you work to establish your collaborative relationship, consider the guiding questions in figure 6.1. Use these questions as discussion points as you begin to determine how your relationship can develop to help you meet the learning goals for your students.

Use the guiding questions not only to prompt discussions, but to consider how you might move closer to achieving your ideal relationship. We suggest you begin by looking over the entire list while each of you mark the three to five most important questions, those you wonder the most about. Eventually, you will want to cover the majority of questions, but start small and build up your knowledge base about one another by going deeper, not wider.

Figure 6.1: Guiding questions to build a relationship.

Guiding Questions	Me	My Partner	Our Ideal
What role assumptions do we bring to our partnership?			
How do we define our students?			
How do we define our own teaching styles?			
What is my preferred work/organizational style?			
What expertise, strengths, and resources do we bring to the partnership?			
What challenges, fears, concerns, and resistance will we need to overcome to be successful in our collaborations?			
What are we likely to whine about?			
How can we ensure that we openly share and stay fully engaged and present in our collaborative work?			
What process will we use to establish our expectations, learn what we need to know about one another, and what we need to do in order to feel safe, grow, and improve as a collaborative team?			

How can we be assured that it is safe to take the necessary risks while we experiment with our shared practice?			
Can we teach together?			
Where would you like to begin?			
How might we complement one another?			
How will we ensure that both of us are actively engaged and neither of us feels over- or underutilized?			
Do we both have the same level of expertise about the curriculum and instruction of general education students? Of special education students? Of students with other issues?			
How do I feel about teaching students with special needs in a general education classroom?			
A problem I foresee as possibly happening in a co-taught classroom is . . .			

Visit **go.solution-tree.com/specialneeds** to download and print this figure.

Sharing a Vision—*Relationship-Building Protocol*

It may be just an urban legend, but the old adage says it very well:

A vision without a plan is just a dream.
A plan without a vision is just drudgery.
But a vision with a plan can change the world.

A shared vision does many things, including:

- Creates the future

- Identifies the need to work together

- Establishes the legitimacy of collaboration

- Enables both parties to enlist others in their efforts

- Develops a sense of urgency

- Defines options and resources

- Helps develop shared accountability

- Asks, "How will the learning be improved?"

Co-teachers and collaborators would do well to come to consensus on core values such as fairness and rigor. Establishing ethical boundaries of your teaching partnerships will help you find common ground on a host of decisions and situations that will mark the day-to-day workings for your shared practice.

Your shared vision might address such topics as shared values and beliefs about students, learning, and your teaching responsibilities, or your commitment to your profession as an educator. Other elements might include shared resources, respect, communication, and other important expectations.

Using this visioning protocol, you and your partner can begin to create the kind of collaborative environment and teaching and learning that you believe will help all students achieve to the best of their abilities. Many partners skip this part of the collaborative process. Unfortunately, they question the value of doing so when the day-to-day problems they are facing seem so overwhelming. We have found that just as problem solving is important, so too is visioning. Both processes should be used in tandem for maximum success.

If you create a vision, you both work toward a common goal, hope, and a positive view of the future. You have a sense of helping determine how you move forward. You have hope that there can be a better way. You can generate a creative plan and engage the passions that you are committed to. You are more in control of the situation.

If you only work together in order to solve problems, you can get stuck before you even correctly define the problem, or you can get mired down in concerns that keep you from dealing with the real issues. Indeed, as useful as problem solving can be, it is usually always reactionary, and rarely leads to fundamental or lasting change.

We commonly think of problems as negatives to avoid; on the other hand, visions conjure up ideas of positive movement to a desired goal.

With your partner, take some time to ask the following questions:

- What would our students experience if we had the power to plan their learning experiences any way we wanted?
- What would the ideal learning environment look like?
- What experiences could we provide that would best prepare students for successful adulthood?
- Who could we ask to join us as learning collaborators in this endeavor?
- How would we assess our students?
- How would we continue to grow as professionals?
- How would we know we were successful?

After brainstorming your responses to these questions, each of you can attempt to make a positive, declarative one-sentence statement about your vision of the future educational experience for your students.

Write each of your statements on a piece of paper and share with one another. Your goal is not to wordsmith a shared vision, but to find a statement that reflects your combined thinking about what you hope for your shared students. You might find it helpful to group the elements of the vision into some common themes such as grading, environment, instructional planning, and so on. Be careful to include all of the elements that it would take to make your vision a reality.

Be as creative as you want as you formulate your common vision statement. It can be a list of ideas, simple text, in graphic form, photos, a mind map, or other images. By simply agreeing on a shared vision, you are on your way to a more successful collaborative experience.

Pondering the Practicalities— *Processing Protocol*

After getting to know one another and clarifying a shared vision, it is helpful for co-teachers and teams to begin to tackle the practical day-to-day issues that will get you started in your collaborations. The topics in figure 6.2 come from conversations among hundreds of teachers as they began those same collaborations.

It is always smart to be proactive and lay our assumptions aside, otherwise these issues tend to surface well after partners have begun teaching together. We encourage you to see how many of these practicalities you can come to agreement on before your teaching assignments begin. Scan the entire list in figure 6.2 with your partner, and then prioritize the three or four items you feel are the most critical as you begin.

Comparing which items each of you identified will be important. Did you choose the same things, or were all of your choices different? After you have had enough time to jot down notes about how you value each of the items, share with your partner. If an item is not going to be an issue in your co-teaching, move to the next item. There is no need to spend time on items you agree on or do not see as problematic. If you get stuck on differences, look for common ground. As you gradually work through the relevant items from the whole list, you will find you have proactively eliminated many of your potential barriers to success.

Critical conversations sets 2 and 3 will further inform your understanding of your students, goals, and strategies, but it is never too early to begin thinking about how your collaborative relationships will ultimately improve the instruction you deliver for your students. Your co-teaching opportunities are a perfect platform to change the way you may have thought about support for your students. Rather than the far too typical "yours and mine" mentality, co-teaching offers a context to help your school become more of a unified system with multiple avenues for all students to be successful. Avoid the yours-and-mine mentality by being intentional in establishing a collaborative environment, deciding on groupings of students, creating a spirit of inclusiveness versus separateness, and modeling joint ownership of materials, space, and other resources. Evidence of parity is more apparent to students and outsiders than you may think, and it demands some intentional planning as well. And in the process, you can use your collaborative partnership as an opportunity for professional growth while having fun as you see the synergy that can come from your joint efforts.

Figure 6.2: Practicalities rating exercise.

____ 1. Developing effective collaboration processes for planning, decision making, and problem solving

____ 2. Designing learning goals and outcomes evident to all partners

____ 3. Using reflective dialogue to plan quality instruction, make decisions, solve problems, discuss student issues, and improve shared practice by learning from one another

____ 4. Focusing on instructional preparation and delivery

____ 5. Designing lessons that are differentiated in content, process, product, and learning environment

____ 6. Incorporating teaching strategies while assisting and monitoring all students and using multiple groupings

____ 7. Using assessments wisely and throughout the learning process (both pre and post)

____ 8. Using a variety of co-teaching models: complementary, side by side, and teaming

____ 9. Providing consistent and clear procedures and routines, and consistent implementation to ensure successful classroom management

____ 10. Deciding on a fair and equitable grading system

____ 11. Providing a high degree of student engagement (participation matched to instruction and preassessment)

____ 12. Integrating age-appropriate technology

Visit **go.solution-tree.com/specialneeds** *to download and print this figure.*

When we refer to content, we mean much more than a textbook or series of lessons in a particular discipline. In our concept of content both teachers have a shared understanding of all curriculum, instruction, and assessment policies and procedures. They also demonstrate regular use of evidence-based instructional strategies and align their daily planning and instructional delivery with professional standards and relevant and appropriate district, state, and national initiatives.

The teaching processes include the bulk of the collaborative work. These processes are designed to get the most out of your collaboration and also to provide a reasonable return on investment for your school district. There was a time when special educators and resources followed students around. Now, we have come to understand that it is far more efficient and effective to put our resource emphasis on our instruction, as opposed to individual students. We do this by implementing a wide variety of creative and collaborative instructional strategies and student groupings.

Determining Roles, Responsibilities, and Processes —
Processing Protocol

Now that you have gotten to know one another, begun to clarify your shared vision for co-teaching, and determined many of the pragmatics of getting started, it is time to determine the roles and responsibilities you will share in this new venture.

Reflect individually on each of the roles and responsibilities you currently have, using figure 6.3. Add to your list any new responsibilities you expect to be held accountable for as a result of this partnership. You might want to jot down some notes and talking points about your reflections to use as you and your partner share your lists. Use this conversation to help you begin to determine which roles and responsibilities each of you will handle as you design your co-teaching partnership.

Figure 6.3: Roles, responsibilities, and processes reflection.

	Talking Points for Awareness and Understanding	Our Agreements
At present, my responsibilities include: I would be willing to share the following responsibilities:		
I would be willing to give up the following responsibilities:		
Consequences of changing my current roles and responsibilities might include:		
Obstacles I believe we would need to address include:		
Ideally, I would like to be assigned the following roles and responsibilities in this new partnership:		

	Talking Points for Awareness and Understanding	Our Agreements
How might our previous conversations about ourselves and our vision help shape the way we decide on our roles and responsibilities?		

*Visit **go.solution-tree.com/specialneeds** to download and print this figure.*

SPECIAL OCCASION CONVERSATIONS

Setting Our Norms— *Processing Protocol*

All educators in co-teaching partnerships must pay attention to content (learning goals and outcomes) and process if they are to be successful. Processes include the various ways that partners communicate with each other and how they hold each other accountable for moving the project forward and accomplishing the goals.

Many school teams establish norms or ground rules, but often partners feel that such rules are not necessary if there are just two or three co-teachers working together. We strongly urge you to take the time to establish these norms. As with all of the protocols in our framework, this process of setting norms can prove invaluable in moving your efforts forward in positive and growth-producing ways. Partners who do not take the time to create norms often find themselves spinning their wheels in wasted meetings, showing disrespect to one another, or worse.

Norms provide a clear focus on the way we do our business together. Partners agree on what is important to each of them. Perhaps being on time is the most important thing to Cindy, and Susie is more concerned with making sure that each partner has veto power over any decisions. Whatever the norms you decide on (usually three to five will suffice), you will find that your process runs much more smoothly with these guidelines in place.

Following are sample process norms other co-teaching partners have used. After reviewing these, brainstorm your own list and narrow it down to three to five norms:

- Treat each other with respect.
- Be transparent.
- Be genuine.
- Challenge one another.
- Trust each other.
- Keep confidences.
- Make sure each of our voices is heard.
- Listen first to understand.
- Be open minded.
- Give our colleagues the benefit of the doubt.
- Be accountable and responsible to our partnership.
- Come prepared to all meetings and classes.

Special Occasion Conversations

Make sure you review the list before each of your meetings and planning sessions as you are learning to work together. Just as important, after each conversation, check in with one another to make sure you honored the intent of your norms. You will also want to revisit and revise them occasionally.

Though not unique, another version of group norms is quite simple and easy to remember. This is a frequent default version for many co-teaching partners:

- Respect one another.
- Respect our students.
- Respect our work together.

What are the norms under which your partnership will operate?

Getting the DIRT on One Another—*Relationship-Building Protocol*

One way to get to know one another is to explore learning styles, work preferences, and other idiosyncrasies so that you can be more effective and efficient in your collaborations. Several instruments are available to help you get to know one another. We include a reproducible copy of the DIRT Temperament Survey as an example (fig. 6.4). There are many other common self- and partner assessments. We are particularly fond of DIRT (widely available for no cost on the Internet), Kaleidoscope, True Colors, and the 4MAT teaching style inventory.

Figure 6.4: DIRT temperament survey.

Directions: Circle one word in each row that you feel is the best description of you, given the choices in that line. Go with your first instincts. Try to avoid overanalyzing your responses. If you tend to think in terms of contexts, use your school environment to frame your responses.

#	A	B	C	D
1	Restrained	Forceful	Careful	Expressive
2	Pioneering	Correct	Emotional	Satisfied
3	Willing	Animated	Bold	Precise
4	Stubborn	Bashful	Indecisive	Unpredictable
5	Respectful	Outgoing	Patient	Determined
6	Persuasive	Self-reliant	Cooperative	Gentle
7	Cautious	Even tempered	Decisive	Life of the party
8	Popular	Assertive	Perfectionist	Generous
9	Unpredictable	Bashful	Indecisive	Argumentative
10	Agreeable	Optimistic	Persistent	Accommodating
11	Positive	Humble	Neighborly	Talkative
12	Friendly	Obliging	Playful	Strong willed
13	Charming	Adventurous	Disciplined	Consistent
14	Soft spoken	Dry humor	Aggressive	Attractive
15	Enthusiastic	Analytical	Sympathetic	Determined
16	Bossy	Inconsistent	Slow	Critical
17	Sensitive	Force of character	Spirited	Laid back

#	A	B	C	D
18	Influential	Kind	Independent	Orderly
19	Idealistic	Popular	Cheerful	Outspoken
20	Impatient	Moody	Aimless	Show off
21	Competitive	Spontaneous	Loyal	Thoughtful
22	Self-Sacrificing	Considerate	Convincing	Courageous
23	Fearful	Changeable	Pessimistic	Tactless
24	Tolerant	Conventional	Stimulating	Resourceful

Visit **go.solution-tree.com/specialneeds** to download and print this figure.

After you have marked your responses, use the scoring sheet (fig. 6.5) to score your survey. On each line across, circle the letter that coincides with the response you made for that line on the survey. When you have circled all of your responses, total the number of circles for each of the columns, and write those numbers on the last space on each of the columns. The largest numbers are the roles that you most generally favor in your interactions. The smallest numbers represent your least favorite roles.

Figure 6.5: DIRT scoring sheet.

Name:

Refer to your survey answers, and mark the letter that corresponds with the column of the word that you circled for each of the twenty-four items. Add your totals for each column to find your preferences.

#	Doer	Influencer	Relater	Thinker
1	B	D	A	C
2	A	C	D	B
3	C	B	A	D
4	A	D	C	B
5	D	B	C	A
6	B	A	D	C
7	C	D	B	A
8	B	A	D	C
9	D	A	C	B
10	C	B	D	A
11	A	D	C	B
12	D	C	A	B
13	B	A	D	C
14	C	D	B	A
15	D	A	C	B
16	A	B	C	D

continued →

Special Occasion Conversations

#	Doer	Influencer	Relater	Thinker
17	B	C	D	A
18	C	A	B	D
19	D	B	C	A
20	A	D	C	B
21	A	B	C	D
22	D	C	B	A
23	D	B	A	C
24	D	C	A	B
Totals				

Visit **go.solution-tree.com/specialneeds** *to download and print this figure.*

The charts in figures 6.6 and 6.7 will help you interpret the roles. When you are finished reading and discussing your collective scores, note some strategies your team might consider based on the DIRT you have on one another.

Because this is an informal and unscientific instrument, don't read too much into the interpretations. Think of the categories as conversation prompts to help you and your partner or team clarify differences and deal with possible implications of those differences. Together you can decide whether you agree with your findings and how the information might inform your collaborative work.

Figure 6.6: Understanding DIRT roles.

Understanding Doers		Understanding Influencers	
Basic motivation	Results and challenge	Basic motivation	Recognition and approval
Best environment	Continual challenge, freedom to act, variety	Best environment	Friendly atmosphere, freedom from control and detail, opportunity to influence others
Accepts/rejects	Accepts the difficult, rejects inaction	Accepts/rejects	Accepts involvement with others, rejects isolation
Major strengths	Getting things done, decisiveness, persistence	Major strengths	Optimism, personable nature, enthusiasm
Weaknesses	Insensitive to others, impatient, overlooks risks and facts	Weaknesses	Overselling, manipulative, lacks follow-through
Behavior under tension	Inflexible, unyielding, autocratic	Behavior under tension	Attacks
Would benefit from . . .	Listening	Would benefit from . . .	Pausing, commitment to moving forward

Understanding Relaters		Understanding Thinkers	
Basic motivation	Relationships and appreciation	Basic motivation	To be right, quality
Best environment	Specialization, working with a group, consistency	Best environment	Supportive and predictable, clearly defined, requiring precision
Accepts/rejects	Accepts friendship, rejects conflict	Accepts/rejects	Accepts methods, rejects lack of quality
Major strengths	Supportive, agreeable, loyal	Major strengths	Orderly, thorough, analytical
Weaknesses	Conforming, retiring, misses opportunities	Weaknesses	Picky, too detailed, too cautious
Behavior under tension	Acquiesces	Behavior under tension	Avoids
Would benefit from . . .	Initiating	Would benefit from . . .	Declaring

*Visit **go.solution-tree.com/specialneeds** to download and print this figure.*

Figure 6.7: Understanding temperament summary.

	Doers	Influencers	Relaters	Thinkers
Value to a team	Takes initiative	Influences people	Builds relationships	Focuses on details
Motivated by	Results, challenge, action	Recognition, approval, vanity	Relationships, appreciation	Being right, quality
Time management	Focuses on now, uses time efficiently, likes to get to the point	Focuses on the future, tends to rush to the next exciting thing	Focuses on the present, spends time in personal interaction	Focuses on the past, works more slowly to ensure accuracy
Communications	One way—not as good at listening, better at initiating communication	Enthusiastic, stimulating, often one-way, can inspire others	Two-way flow, a good listener	Good listener, especially in relation to tasks
Emotional response	Detached, independent	Highs and lows, excitable	Warm, friendly	Sensitive, careful
Decision making	Impulsive, makes decisions without goal in mind	Intuitive and quick, lots of wins and losses	Relational, makes decisions more slowly due to input from others	Reluctant, thorough, needs lots of evidence
Behavior under tension	Autocratic	Attacks	Acquiesces	Avoids

*Visit **go.solution-tree.com/specialneeds** to download and print this figure.*

Special Occasion Conversations

Solving Our Problems—*Processing Protocol*

Collaboration is a superior way of solving a problem during a meeting or change effort. However, a number of conditions need to be in place to ensure a successful outcome if your collaboration is to be successful. Partners or members of a team must:

- Have sufficient trust among them to open up and be supportive of each other when necessary
- Have a positive intent to work toward a win-win solution
- Have relevant information on hand to make a sound decision
- Have the time to make these decisions
- Believe the topic is important enough to warrant spending the time it will take

This activity (fig. 6.8) has the best results when each partner self-reflects on how well he or she individually handles conflict before sharing with his or her partner. We have provided a few prompts to follow. Compare and use the information about your similarities and differences to help inform your processes of collaboration.

The first prompt asks you to rate your ability to handle stress and conflict. Then you will be asked to provide a few words describing recent conflicts in your own life as well as responses if you have gotten angry. Following that segment, you will be given a list of suggested norms to help you and your partner use as you become more creative in solving conflicting situations. This protocol concludes with a short section on mediation as a creative solution to challenges.

It's important to remember that conflict does not necessarily have to be negative. Conflict can have positive effects and outcomes, such as the following. It can:

- Demonstrate that diverse stakeholders are involved.
- Uncover interests.
- Deepen our understanding of a problem.
- Provide more options for action.
- Be about learning instead of winning or losing.
- Build group confidence.

The following norms have been created to help you approach your conflicts with more creative responses. When we think proactively and increase our repertoire for responding, we can avoid the unpleasantness that sometimes ensues when tempers flare or when we are too stressed to remain unemotional. Co-teaching partners generally have developed processes to help them handle the issues they haven't anticipated, but we are all human, so disputes do arise from time to time. Together, consider how each of the following norms might be adopted by your partnership or develop your own explicit process to use when problems and challenges do arise. Only rarely do partners find themselves in a situation they cannot handle without mediation. We have suggestions for that possibility as well.

As with any time you establish norms, they should be developed by the people who are going to be using them. We offer these as a good starting point as you decide the norms that will work for you:

- Value and incorporate diversity.
- Create a safe environment for difference.

Figure 6.8: Solving our problems.

Rate your ability to handle problems by circling a number from one to five.				
1	2	3	4	5
Poorly—I get very upset. I run from conflict. I blow up.				Very Well—I can use conflict constructively.

Most of us can easily think of conflicts in our lives, even in the last week or two.

Think of three situations of conflict that have occurred in your life recently.

1.

2.

3.

Did any of these conflicts bring benefits? If so, what were they?

Could they have been more beneficial? How?

For each of the situations, is there anything you wish you had done differently?

An easy question: Can you think of two or three times recently when you have felt anger? Write them down.

A tougher question: If you are not satisfied with how you handled your anger, what would your improved behavior have looked like?

*Visit **go.solution-tree.com/specialneeds** to download and print this figure.*

- Agree to leave labels at the door.
- Agree to disagree, and then explore common ground.
- Keep the focus on the present, and on the solutions.
- Discipline expressions of anger.
- Be well prepared.
- Make no permanent enemies.
- Model the surfacing of conflict.

Considering this information about conflict, address the following points:

1 Which of the how-tos of creative conflict do you most need to practice during the coming week in your school, district, or community?

2 Develop a plan of action. What specifically are you going to do in order to practice creative conflict during the next week? What benefits do you expect? How will you know if you've succeeded (or at least made progress)?

3 Share your plan of action with a colleague to get honest, helpful feedback about your plan. Note any issues, topics, or reflection "gems" that you want to capture from your discussions.

Special Occasion Conversations

Should your team or partnership be unable to resolve issues, you have a number of options. Mediation is the last intrusive intervention, and it is also easiest when people are eager to resolve their differences. Mediation can help you to avoid destructive conflict, it helps simplify the situation and makes it easier to problem solve, and it can reduce the likelihood that you will have repeated conflicts. Primarily, mediation offers a way to move beyond the difficult issues with personal dignity and mutual respect intact.

During mediation, someone who is neutral—the mediator—invites those in conflict to state their views. This can involve a panel of people. The mediator listens in order to bring differences to the surface. The mediator doesn't judge, but asks questions to uncover common interests. He or she then stresses points in common that disputants may not see. The disputants talk directly to each other to search for a win-win solution that meets some interests of both parties. This negotiation has some specific benefits. It:

- Makes problem solving and resolution more possible
- Maintains the dignity of all parties
- Makes it more likely that agreements will be upheld
- Reduces the likelihood of the need for problem solving in the future, and helps prepare the ground for it should it happen

It is helpful to remember a few key points in order to put these strategies to good use:

- Know your interests so well that you know what you can compromise.
- Focus on critical interests; don't get bogged down in debate over means.
- Search for common interests; work to narrow differences.
- Maintain respectful communication—it's in your interest.
- Take the pressure off, and keep talking.

Finally you and your partner can use the information in this protocol as a foundation when you are facing challenges, conflicts, or disagreements. Considering the information about mediation and negotiation, address the following questions:

1 Think of the three disputes you listed earlier (in fig. 6.8) that you have observed in the recent past. Could a mediator have helped?

2 What might mediation have offered you in each of these conflicts?

3 What about your role in mediation? What could you have done to facilitate the reaching of a constructive agreement?

Managing Our Conflicts — *Relationship-Building Protocol*

Have you ever wondered whether you and your partner could weather a conflict? Have you ever failed in your attempt to settle a dispute at school? Do you want to increase the repertoire of tools and resources you and your partner might use to avoid major conflicts and to help your relationship run more smoothly? This conversation provides a series of tools and resources to help you and your partner become more skilled at settling differences. You will first want to look through all of the instruments offered in this protocol and decide where to begin if you have a particular situation you want to resolve. Otherwise, we suggest you work through to familiarize yourself with all of the instruments and talk about how they might be useful in particular situations.

First, we offer some thought provokers to help you gear up for the exercises that follow:

1 What are the most common conflicts you are likely to have to deal with at school?

2 What are some typical responses you have when you are stressed?

3 What strategies do you typically employ to deal with stressful situations?

4 Are these the same strategies you would use to deal with stress in other areas of your life outside of school?

5 Would you consider conflict and stress to be negative factors for you?

We tend to think of *conflict* as a negative, but that is not necessarily so; we have imposed that negative connotation. A little insight into how we are apt to handle stress or conflict helps us become more aware of how we frame discussions so that our conversations can be more positive or negative. How we set the tone of our initial invitations for others to join us can have a huge bearing on how well they are received. Being intentional and positive can even help avoid real difficulties. With your partner, discuss the conflict management approaches featured in figure 6.9 that people typically use. Focus your discussion on how using each of these strategies might affect your partnership.

Figure 6.9: Conflict-management approaches.

Avoidance

When you avoid difficult situations, you are not dealing with the issues. Use avoidance strategies only in those few situations when issues can't be resolved profitably.

Accommodation

When you accommodate, you are just smoothing things over. Use this approach only in those few situations where keeping the peace is of more importance than finding a solution.

Competition

Competing divides groups and creates a win-lose mentality. This is a no-win situation for educators and facilitators because it has zero percent applicability.

Compromising

Compromising finds the middle ground. Use this approach in situations where you are faced with polarized choices.

Collaborating

Collaborating gets people working together to find the best solution for everyone. This is the preferred approach for all groups for most disputes. Use it in conflict situations.

Creative conflict resolution, mediation, and negotiation are valuable tools to help groups settle their differences.

Talking About Identity and Integrity—*Reflecting Protocol*

This conversation will help you and your partner explore your identity and integrity as teachers. If you have not read Parker Palmer's book (1998) *The Courage to Teach: Exploring the Inner Landscape of a Teacher's Life*, we hope you will pick up a copy soon. We have developed this protocol based on his work. Over the years, many of the co-teachers we have worked with reported profound effects from reflecting on their identity and integrity as teachers.

Palmer (1998, 2000, 2004) encourages us to ask questions that honor and challenge the teacher's heart. These questions invite a deeper inquiry than our traditional conversations. In large part, our conversations focus on the "What?" questions: What do I do as a professional? What subjects shall we teach? When the conversation goes a bit deeper, we get at the "How?" questions: How do we teach well? What methods and techniques are required to teach well? Occasionally, when the conversation goes deeper still, we ask the "Why?" question: For what purpose and to what ends do we teach? Seldom, if ever, do we ask the "Who?" questions: Who is the self that teaches? How do I describe my identity and integrity as a teacher? (Palmer, 1998).

Palmer asks us to consider how the quality of our selfhood forms or informs the way we relate to our students, our subjects, our colleagues, and our world. We can use his prompts to help us consider how educational institutions can sustain and deepen the selfhood from which good teaching comes.

As important as our teaching methods may be, the most practical thing we can achieve in *any* kind of work is insight into what is happening inside of us as we do our work. Palmer believes that technique is what we use until "the real teacher arrives."

The *courage to teach*, according to Palmer, is "the courage to keep one's heart open in those very moments when the heart is asked to hold more than it is able so that teacher and students and subject can be woven into the fabric of community that learning and living requires" (1998, p. 11). Good teaching comes from the identity and the integrity of the teacher. Palmer tells us that "if we want to grow as teachers, we must do something alien to academic culture: we must talk to each other about our inner lives—risky stuff in a profession that fears the personal and seeks safety in the technical, the distant, and the abstract" (p. 12). Palmer reminds us that especially when we are just beginning to teach, but often for a long time, we easily fall back on the strategies and activities we have picked up in our training. It takes us a while to come into our own as teachers, to integrate who we are with what we do in the classroom. He points out the following paradoxes (1998, p. 68):

- We separate head from heart.
  - This results in minds that don't know how to feel, and hearts that don't know how to think.
- We separate facts from feelings.
  - This results in an abundance of facts that make the world distant and remote, and ignorant emotions that reduce truth to how one feels today.
- We separate theory from practice.
  - This results in theories that have little to do with life, and practice that is uninformed by understanding.
- We separate teaching from learning.
  - This results in teachers who talk but do not listen, and students who listen but do not talk.

Deepening partner and team conversations can help us address these paradoxes as we begin to design collaborative teaching and learning spaces.

Ask yourselves and your partner the following questions: What is it we do? What defines our space? What is our work or profession? What organizations are we affiliated with?

When you have begun to clarify your own identity and integrity as teachers and as partners, begin to listen intently to your colleagues. You might choose to listen at the next faculty meeting or in the lunchroom. Try a grade-level or department meeting or even a districtwide textbook adoption committee meeting or a PTO meeting. When you listen intently, you can tell a lot about the identity and integrity of colleagues, depending on the conversation. Palmer says we talk very little about who we are, and we edge further out of the circles as we share with colleagues. But he reminds us that until we bring the *who* into our work, we are only going through the motions. We must go deeper to get the really important "Who?" conversations.

Explore ways that you and your partner might invite more meaningful conversations with colleagues as you explore the inner landscape of your lives as teachers. Explore ways that you might create collaborative spaces such as Palmer suggests, spaces that are bounded and open; hospitable and "charged"; inviting to the voice of the individual and the voice of the group; honoring of the "little" stories of the students and the "big" stories of the disciplines and tradition; supportive of solitude and surrounded by the resources of community; and welcoming of both silence and speech.

We designed figure 6.10 to help teachers listen more intently to the kinds of information they were sharing with one another. In hundreds of trainings, as teachers introduced one another and shared key information they had heard from their colleagues, we stuck colored dots on a huge bull's-eye to denote whether each of the points of information belonged to the What, How, Why, or Who circles. Generally there were lots of dots on the outer edges of the bull's-eye, with far fewer in the middle—the heart of teaching, according to Palmer. Granted, this kind of activity is a bit artificial and contrived, but it does help us remember that we have so little precious time to relate to one another in meaningful ways, that it behooves us to make the most of those times. The sooner we can get to the issues that really concern our identity and integrity as teachers, the sooner we will align our practices with our deeper meaning as individuals and as educators. When teachers have gone through this activity with us, they have reported that they hear their colleagues in deeper and more meaningful ways.

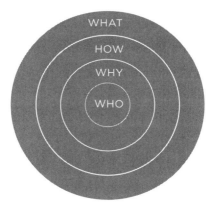

Adapted from Palmer, 1998, 2000, 2004.

Figure 6.10: Identity and integrity graphic.

Being Willing to Be Disturbed—*Reflecting Protocol*

Are we willing to be disturbed as we look forward to changes in the way we teach?

Silently read the following passage taken from Margaret Wheatley's (2002) *Turning to One Another*. When you have finished reading the passage, discuss the prompts at the end of this protocol with your partner to help you determine how willing you both are to change the ways to which you have grown accustomed.

Willing to Be Disturbed, Margaret Wheatley

As we work together to restore hope to the future, we need to include a new and strange ally—our willingness to be disturbed. Our willingness to have our beliefs and ideas challenged by what others think. No one person or perspective can give us the answers we need to the problems of today. Paradoxically, we can only find those answers by admitting we don't know. We have to be willing to let go of our certainty and expect ourselves to be confused for a time.

We weren't trained to admit we don't know. Most of us were taught to sound certain and confident, to state our opinion as if it were true. We haven't been rewarded for being confused. Or for asking more questions rather than giving quick answers. We've also spent many years listening to others mainly to determine whether we agree with them or not. We don't have time or interest to sit and listen to those who think differently than we do.

But the world now is quite perplexing. We no longer live in those sweet, slow days when life felt predictable, when we actually knew what to do next. We live in a complex world, we often don't know what's going on, and we won't be able to understand the complexity unless we spend more time in not knowing.

It is very difficult to give up our certainties—our positions, our beliefs, our explanations. These help define us: they lie at the heart of our personal identity. Yet I believe we will succeed in changing this world only if we can think and work together in new ways. Curiosity is what we need. We don't have to let go of what we believe, but we do need to be curious about what someone else believes. We do need to acknowledge that their way of interpreting the world might be essential to our survival.

We live in a dense and tangled global system. Because we live in different parts of this complexity, and because no two people are physically identical, we each experience life differently. It's impossible for any two people to ever see things exactly the same. You can test this out for yourself. Take any event that you've shared with others (a speech, a movie, a current event, a major problem) and ask your colleagues and friends to describe their interpretation of that event. I think you'll be amazed at how many different explanations you'll hear. Once you get a sense of the diversity, try asking even more colleagues. You'll end up with a rich tapestry of interpretations that are much more interesting than any single one.

To be curious about how someone interprets things, we have to be willing to admit that we're not capable of figuring things out alone. If our solutions don't work as well as we want them to, if our explanations of why something happened don't feel sufficient, it's time to begin asking others about what they see and think. When so many interpretations are available, I can't understand why we would be satisfied with superficial conversations where we pretend to agree with one another.

There are many ways to sit and listen for the differences. Lately, I've been listening for what surprises me. What did I just hear that startled me? This isn't easy—I'm accustomed to sitting there nodding my head to those saying things I agree with. But when I notice what surprises me, I'm able to see my own views more clearly, including my beliefs and assumptions.

Noticing what surprises and disturbs me has been a very useful way to see invisible beliefs. If what you say surprises me, I must have been assuming something else was true. If what you say disturbs me, I must believe something contrary to you. My shock at your position exposes my own position. When I hear myself saying, "how could anyone believe something like that?" a light comes on for me to see my own beliefs. These moments are great gifts. If I can see my beliefs and assumptions, I can decide whether I still value them.

I hope you'll begin a conversation, listening for what's new. Listen as best you can for what's different, for what surprises you. See if this practice helps you learn something new. Notice whether you develop a better relationship with the person you're talking with. If you try this with several people, you might find yourself laughing in delight as you realize how many unique ways there are to be human.

We have the opportunity many times a day, every day, to be the one who listens to others, curious rather than certain. But the greatest benefit of all is that listening moves us closer. When we listen with less judgment, we always develop better relationships with each other. It's not differences that divide us. It's our judgments about each other that do. Curiosity and good listening bring us back together.

Sometimes we hesitate to listen for differences because we don't want to change. We're comfortable with our lives, and if we listened to anyone who raised questions, we'd have to get engaged in changing things. If we don't listen, things can stay as they are and we won't have to expend any energy. But most of us do see things in our life or in the world that we would like to be different. If that's true, we have to listen more, not less. And we have to be willing to move into the very uncomfortable place of uncertainty.

We can't be creative if we refuse to be confused. Change always starts with confusion; cherished interpretations must dissolve to make way for the new. Of course it's scary to give up what we know, but the abyss is where newness lives. Great ideas and inventions miraculously appear in the space of not knowing. If we can move through the fear and enter the abyss, we are rewarded greatly. We discover that we're creative.

As the world grows more strange and puzzling and difficult, I don't believe most of us want to keep struggling through it alone. I can't know what to do from my own narrow perspective. I know I need a better understanding of what's going on. I want to sit down with you and talk about all of the frightening and hopeful things I observe, and listen to what frightens you and gives you hope. I need new ideas and solutions for the problems I care about. I know I need to talk to you to discover those. I need to learn to value your perspective, and I want you to value mine. I expect to be disturbed by what I hear from you. I know we don't have to agree with each other in order to think well together. There is no need for us to be joined at the ear. We are joined by our human hearts. (Wheatley, 2002, pp. 34–37)

Reflect on the words and phrases that resonated with you.
Share your initial thoughts and reactions with your partner.
Ask each other the following questions:

- Are you willing to be disturbed, to go out of your own comfort zone as you begin to collaborate together?

- If you are not willing to be disturbed, what are the implications for your partnership?

- What are the expectations and concerns you feel in this process?

- How might you find a way through the doubt and uneasiness to actually become disturbed enough to find a new way in the world of your work?

Getting Fierce — *Communicating Protocol*

This protocol is designed to give you and your partner the opportunity to review the seven principles of fierce conversations and see if they have relevance to your personal and professional success. In *Fierce Conversations*, Susan Scott (2002) offers these principles to consider when you prepare for difficult conversations:

1 Master the courage to interrogate reality.

2 Come out from behind yourself, into the conversation, and make it real.

3 Be here, prepared to be nowhere else.

4 Tackle your toughest challenge today.

5 Obey your instincts.

6 Take responsibility for your emotional wake.

7 Let silence do the heavy lifting.

Scott says that accountability is the single most powerful, most desired, yet least understood characteristic of a high-performance culture. It's an attitude, a private, non-negotiable choice about how to live one's life. It is a choice that makes all the difference. The problem is that holding people accountable generates tension, yet without accountability, time and energy are spent generating excuses about why something did or did not happen. While it is human nature to blame other people or circumstances for our problems, individuals and organizations pay a high price for this behavior. They adopt strategies that are half-hearted, safe, passive, and diluted. Worse yet, sometimes the result is no action at all.

Scott has designed Mineral Rights as a process to give one of the greatest gifts we can give another person: the purity of our attention. This exercise allows you to mine your relationship for greater clarity, improved understanding, and impetus for change.

With your partner facilitate a conversation using the following steps (Scott, 2002, pp. 83–84). When you are finished, be sure to debrief the process together. Ask your collaborating partner to do the following, and listen carefully to his or her responses.

Step 1   Identify your most pressing issue as it relates to collaboration or co-teaching.

Step 2   Clarify the issue.

Step 3   Determine the current impact.

Step 4   Determine the future implications.

Step 5   Examine your personal contribution to this issue.

Step 6   Describe the ideal outcome.

Step 7   Commit to action.

To get even deeper into the dialogue, following are question prompts to explore with your partner (Scott, p. 221):

1 What's the most important thing we should be talking about today?

2 What topic are you hoping I won't bring up? What topic am I hoping you won't bring up?

3   What do we believe is impossible to do, that if we were able to do it would completely change the game? How can we pull this off?

4   What values do we stand for, and are there gaps between those values and how we actually behave?

5   What is our organization pretending not to know? What are we pretending not to know?

6   How have we behaved in ways guaranteed to produce the results with which we're unhappy?

7   What's the most important decision we're facing? What's keeping us from making it?

8   If we were hired to consult with our colleagues, what advice would we give?

9   If we were competing with our colleagues, what strategy would we use?

10 If nothing changes, what's likely to happen?

11 What are the conversations out there with our names on them—the ones we've been avoiding for days, weeks, months, and years? Who are they with, and what are the topics?

12 Given everything we've explored together, what's the next most potent step we need to take? What's going to try to get in our way? When will we take it? When should we reconnect about how it went and what's next?

These questions will all help you get into deeper dialogue. As your familiarity with and trust in your partner grows and as you learn more about problem-solving approaches, you will be able to gain many benefits from having fierce conversations of your own.

IN A PERFECT WORLD CONVERSATIONS

Sharing Our Personal Bests—*Relationship-Building Protocol*

Reflect on the very best collaborative or co-teaching experience you have been a part of.

Next, write a vivid description of this work, listing the specific qualities that made your experience so successful. Rather than focusing on the chronology of the event or the whole experience, be sure to pinpoint exactly what contributions you personally made to cause the successful outcome.

Then take turns sharing your personal best experiences with your co-teaching partner. Together list three to five qualities that you may have shared in each of your examples, and brainstorm how you might incorporate these qualities to help build your personal best collaborative practice.

Deciding Whether to Intervene—*Assessing Protocol*

When you are aware of your typical reactions to stressful situations, and you and your partner have developed processes to help avoid conflicts but you still get into a bind, there are a few questions you can ask one another to help you decide what your next course of action might be. Ask yourself these questions when deciding if an intervention is advisable:

• Is the problem serious?

• Does it need our attention?

• Can we find the time to address the intervention?

- How much of a disruption will intervening cause?
- How will it impact relationships or interrupt the flow of our work?
- Can the intervention affect our climate?
- Will it damage anyone's self-esteem?
- What's the chance that the intervention will work?
- Do I trust that the situation can be improved?
- Do I have enough credibility to do this, or would someone else do it better?
- Is it appropriate to intervene given the group's level of openness and trust?

Finally, ask one another, "What will happen if we do nothing?"

If your honest dialogue can focus on the answers to these questions, you will have the additional insight as to how to proceed. If the answer is that your partnership will be less effective if you do nothing, you will need to design the best plan to intervene.

Stopping the Conflict Before It Begins — *Processing Protocol*

Have you ever wondered how you might be proactive in avoiding potential conflicts? Have you ever noticed how some colleagues always seem to be in the middle of disputes and others are never involved? Would you like to set a tone that helps you and your partner become more proactive and positive so that you might avoid these difficult situations?

With your partner, read through the list of steps in dealing with difficult situations in figure 6.11. Collaborative partners can create a conflict-friendly foundation for the team by using this approach. The template will help you set the stage for conflict that is creative and productive. Rate where you stand as a pair for each step.

Getting Ready to Co-Teach — *Planning Protocol*

This protocol asks you and your partner to begin at the beginning, even if you have been sharing a practice for some time. By asking yourself and your partner the following questions, you can re-evaluate your readiness, identify issues you may have overlooked, and ensure that your teaching and learning are as efficient and effective as possible.

Figure 6.11: Stopping the Conflict Before It Begins: A self-assessment.

	Not in Place	Partially in Place	In Place and Doing Well
1. Together we set clear goals and expectations for our partnership.			
2. We meet regularly and often.			
3. We get to know one another through frequent interactions that build trust, respect, and confidence.			

	Not in Place	Partially in Place	In Place and Doing Well
4. We assign roles and responsibilities as needed. We consider and take turns serving in a variety of roles, including such responsibilities as being a data collector, the devil's advocate, the pie in the sky, the problem solver, and the convener.			
5. We don't confuse a lack of conflict with agreement.			
6. We actively manage conflict by ensuring that each of our voices is heard, and decisions are made following our agreed-upon process.			
7. We understand our frames of reference. These are the prior experiences we each bring to the situation, our history, assumptions, and past experiences.			
8. We understand our selective perceptions. These are the things we pay particular attention to.			
9. We listen to understand one another. We assert our needs clearly and specifically. We use "I" messages as tools for clarification. We build from what we have heard while continuing to listen well.			
10. To reach common ground, we are both willing to move to higher ground.			
11. When there is an impasse, we are able to manage it with calm, patience, and respect. We do this by clarifying our feelings and focusing on underlying needs, interests, and concerns.			
12. We plan and make doable agreements. First we review what a good agreement would look like, and then we align that with our shared goals and other commitments.			
13. To ensure that we keep our shared commitments to one another, we underpromise and overdeliver when we make those commitments.			

Visit **go.solution-tree.com/specialneeds** to download and print this figure.

In a Perfect World Conversations

Determine the lay of the land:

- What type of collaboration currently exists between general and special education?

- Has there been any discussion of inclusion, collaboration, or co-teaching?

- How do teachers react when they hear about students with special needs in general education classes? Are there any who react favorably?

Tread lightly:

- What is our joint understanding of co-teaching as an effective instructional strategy?

- May I teach or co-teach a lesson with you?

- Which areas do each of you feel are strengths you bring to the relationship, and which areas are likely challenges? How can you merge your own contributions to add value?

Get administrative support:

- How is the district addressing the least restrictive environment (LRE) mandate and the inclusive movement?

- How does the district support collaborative practices?

- What do school data tell us to help us determine which discipline areas or grade levels will begin our collaborative efforts?

- How will we ensure that support is provided across all content areas, including electives?

- Will we have sufficient support to be successful, such as scheduling assistance, common planning time, and so on?

Get to know your partner:

- Do we value the time and energy it will take to get to know one another?

- Are there ways we might pool our content expertise, instructional strategies expertise, and other time, talents, and resources to ensure that we show a return of investment for our collaborative efforts?

- How shall we ensure that we both are actively involved and neither feels over- or underutilized?

- What feedback structure can we create to assist in our regular communication?

- What would a workable schedule look like, and would it meet the needs of the instructors as well as the students we might co-teach?

- How often will co-teaching occur (daily, a few times a week, for a specific unit)?

- How can we ensure that this schedule will be maintained consistently so that both co-teachers can trust it?

- How will we maintain communication between co-taught sessions?

- What professional development opportunities would help inform our collaborative practice?

Reflecting — *Reflecting Protocol*

Read through the following statements, and rank them from one to five, with one signifying total disagreement and five representing total agreement. Feel free to add comments to the ranking, as these comments will help support the conversations with your colleagues. You can use these considerations as reflective journal entries, self-assessments, or starting points for discussions with your partner.

- Overall, I am/have been very satisfied with my collaborative and co-teaching experiences in my current situation.
- I believe that the benefits to our students will outweigh the challenges and extra effort required to make our collaborative practice possible.
- I feel that communication is excellent between my co-teaching colleagues.
- I see strong consistency in the practice and procedures we use in our co-taught or collaborative efforts.
- I feel that each of us adds value to our joint collaborative efforts.
- I feel there is parity in our collaborative relationship.

After ranking these points, suggest one to three things that would improve your relationship. What would they be?

Next, consider how you will measure your success as collaborators.

Talking About Our Talking — *Processing Protocol*

Time is always an issue when you work with others. There is never enough time, and we often find ourselves questioning whether the time we spend in countless meetings is really worth it. When we are able to focus, to improve our listening, and also to discern the outcomes we are being asked to take part in, we can increase our feeling that they are worthwhile.

Discerning the type of conversation we are in is another way to enhance our capacity to listen, make connections, and be in communication with others. We can practice by being silent, reflective, and present in the process. To get smarter about the time we spend in meetings and collaborative endeavors, we offer some prompts to talk about as you decide on whether to meet and how to proceed with your partners:

- What is the purpose, intention, or anticipated outcome of each of our collaborative meetings?
- Why is it important to talk about the topic?
- How can we check out our assumptions?
- Are there structures or protocols that could help facilitate our conversations?
- How will we make decisions?
- How will we creatively troubleshoot and problem solve?

CRITICAL CONVERSATIONS PROTOCOLS: SET 2—EXAMINE DATA

This chapter contains the detailed conversations protocols for set 2, Examine Data. These step-by-step activities will help you and your partner or team develop more effective co-teaching practice. The chapter begins with focus questions and anticipated outcomes and contains three types of conversations: (1) non-negotiable, (2) special occasion, and (3) in a perfect world.

The focus questions will give you an idea of what you'll learn in this set of protocols. The outcomes provide measures to help you determine if you and your partner have covered the kinds of conversations that will help you be successful when you move to the next set. The Reflective Journal (page 46) will help you monitor your progress through the series of protocols.

Visit **go.solution-tree.com/specialneeds** to download the reproducibles for this chapter.

Focus Questions

- What assumptions do we have about our students?
- What relevant school data do we have?
- How can relevant data inform our practice?
- How can we set SMARTER goals to help us meet the diverse instructional needs of and improve achievement for all of our students?

Anticipated Outcomes

- We have clarified our assumptions about our students.
- We have obtained sufficient student and school data.
- We have a process to use relevant data to inform our practice.
- We have set SMARTER goals to help us meet the diverse instructional needs of and improve achievement for all of our students.

Non-Negotiable Conversations

NON-NEGOTIABLE CONVERSATIONS

Moving Beyond Assumptions—*Assessing Protocol*

We have assumptions that we bring to our teaching environment and our relationships with our students and their families. How can we be sure that our assumptions do not lessen our effectiveness as educators? As educators we have a great deal of hard evidence about our students: test scores, attendance, behavior patterns, and so on. We also have many assumptions, given the diverse nature of our classrooms and the differences we see between our students and our experiences as students. It is crucial that you share your assumptions with your collaborators to dispel faulty assumptions and decide together whether you need to gather additional data to ensure you are operating with the best possible understanding of your students. As Garmston and Wellman (1999) describe, "group members need to develop the skills of inquiry to get below the surface" of assumptions (p. 228).

With your partner, begin to tackle the following questions as a way to correct misunderstandings and assumptions about your students and to ensure that the information you have about them is verifiable with evidence. Be creative as you triangulate any particular differences between the real evidence you have and the beliefs and assumptions you may hold. For instance, our grade book evidence shows that some students rarely turn in completed homework. Our teacher assumptions might be that this is because the students just don't care about getting work finished. But if we dig further into other evidence sources about our students, we may actually find that these same students have after-school responsibilities like caring for younger siblings or working into the late evening to help cover family expenses. This new information will help us get a more accurate picture of our students.

The following questions will get you started. Be sure to add others that surface during your discussions that may be relevant to your setting:

- What is it we privately think about our students and their views of the future? How do we think of their families, their values of education?

- How well do we understand the cultural and ethnicity issues that may be different from our own?

- What assumptions do we have as educators that may be determining our effectiveness with our students? How do our assumptions align with the other data we have about our students?

- How can we ensure that we are being culturally competent in our interactions with our students and their families?

Having Picture Day at School—*Assessing Protocol*

As educators, we think we have the real picture of our students, yet many times test scores are the only evidence we seem to consider. How can we get a more comprehensive picture of our students and their abilities, interests, and aptitudes?

Part 1: A Data Picture of Our School

With your partner, gather all of the existing data you have on the students you are teaching. Begin with recent test scores, but also include teacher observations, engagement data, and discipline history.

If your school does not have a comprehensive collection and analysis process, you can use the reproducible chart in figure 7.1, A Data Picture of Our School, which is adapted from *Learning by Doing* (DuFour, DuFour, Eaker, & Many, 2010, pp. 24–25).

Use this complete data picture you have compiled to help inform your collaborative teaching efforts. Guiding questions for you and your co-teaching partner include:

- Are these data being used to help inform all of the decisions being made across the service delivery continuum?

- Which of these data points have the most impact on your collaborative practice? How might you use co-teaching to help address these points?

Most of this information should be readily available. There will inevitably be other data you will want to include or create to complete your picture of each of the students in your school. Talk about the specifics as well as the trends, huge gaps, and other patterns you find.

Figure 7.1: A data picture of our school.

Indicator	Year 20__–20__	Year 20__–20__	Year 20__–20__
School assessment data			
District assessment data			
State assessment data			
National assessment data			
Student engagement data			
Average daily attendance			
Percentage of students using school's tutorial services			
Percentage of students enrolled in most rigorous courses offered			
Percentage of students graduating without retention			
Percentage of students who drop out of school			
Percentage of students engaged in activities in which we hope to engage students, such as community service			
Discipline data			
Number of referrals/top three reasons			

continued →

Indicator	Year 20__-20__	Year 20__-20__	Year 20__-20__
Number of parent conferences relating to discipline			
Number of in-school suspensions			

*Adapted from DuFour et al., 2010, pp. 24–25. Visit **go.solution-tree.com/specialneeds** to download and print this figure.*

Part 2: Professional Learning Community Audit

Use the following PLC audit questions to self- and partner-assess your school climate, and consider how these issues might affect your co-teaching.

- How likely is it for you and your partnership to be successful, given the results of your school or district evidence and your partnership's shared vision?

- What proactive measures might you take to address any discrepancies in the evidence and the desired results you might like to have to be successful?

- What action steps could you and your partner take to address these discrepancies?

- Have you uncovered aspects of your school environment that might prompt you to celebrate, recognize, or acknowledge colleagues?

Richard DuFour, Robert Eaker, Rebecca DuFour, and Tom Many (2010) offer some guiding questions (see fig. 7.2) that may give additional insight on more subtle data that affect our teaching and learning. For each of these questions in the PLC audit, be prepared to share evidence to support your responses.

Figure 7.2: Picture day guiding questions.

Guiding Questions	Evidence From Our School or District	What Our Partnership Plans to Do to Align With Our Shared Vision
What do we plan for?		
What do we monitor?		
What do we model?		
What questions do we ask?		
How do we allocate our resources: time, money, and people?		

Guiding Questions	Evidence From Our School or District	What Our Partnership Plans to Do to Align With Our Shared Vision
What do we celebrate?		
What are we willing to confront?		

*Source: DuFour et al. (2010). Visit **go.solution-tree.com/specialneeds** to download and print this figure.*

Committing — *Goal-Setting Protocol*

As educators, we are frequently swamped with requests for help. Daily we can see unmet needs that demand our attention. If we say yes for too many requests, we tend to get overextended, setting ourselves up for failure when we are unable to keep promises. If we say no, we feel guilty when we cannot help at that time. One way we can help one another is to make realistic commitments with our partners.

When you are setting goals, use the commitments reflection tool in figure 7.3 to help you both be more successful. Partners using this tool find that it helps them to underpromise and overdeliver.

Figure 7.3: Our commitments reflection tool.

Commitments We Will Undertake	Short-Term: By the End of . . .	Mid-Term: By the End of . . .	Long-Term: The Ideals We Hope to Achieve	How We Will Know We Are Successful: Our Indicators, Evidence, and Data	Resources That Will Help Us Succeed
Engaging partners					
Examining data					
Enhancing instruction					
Expanding impact					

*Visit **go.solution-tree.com/specialneeds** to download and print this figure.*

Setting SMARTER Goals — *Goal-Setting Protocol*

We have discovered two variations of the SMART goals familiar to most educators. SMART stands for:

- *Specific*—What are we trying to achieve? What needs to be done? What will it look like?
- *Measureable*—How do we know we achieved it? How many? How frequently? How long from start to finish? Remember, what gets measured gets done.
- *Attainable*—Can it be achieved with current resources and skills? Is it a stretch or a challenge? Aim to stretch.

- *Relevant*—Does the goal or expectation support your vision and mission? How does it link?
- *Time based*—What is the deadline? When will it be achieved? Remember, a goal without a date is a dream.

To make SMARTER goals, try adding an E and an R!

- *Engaging*—Be motivated by it!
- *Reinforcing*—Make sure it supports your values and your emotional commitment to ensure that you achieve the goals.

Talk about your team's goals with your partner. Do you set them yourselves, or are there some from others and some you set yourselves? As you think about setting goals for your collaborative efforts, you will need the SMART components. But do you have something in your goals to address the motivation, the wow factor? The wow factor brings your goals to life. It asks you to remember why it is you are doing what you are doing. It provides the sustaining power of your work. It might be able to sustain you during the difficult times, and give you something to celebrate when you meet your goal.

What are some SMARTER goals you and your partner can agree on?

What is the wow factor to help sustain your pursuit of those goals?

Figure 7.4 will help you organize these goals.

Figure 7.4: SMARTER goals.

Our goal is:	Now let's make sure it is a SMARTER goal!
Specific	
Measureable	
Attainable	
Relevant	
Time based	
Engaging	
Reinforcing	

*Visit **go.solution-tree.com/specialneeds** to download and print this figure.*

Following are some examples of not-so-smart and SMARTER goal statements:

- **Not-so-smart goal statement**—We will take some professional development courses to learn co-teaching strategies.
- **SMARTER goal statement**—By January 1, 2012, we will have researched and decided on a book that we will read and discuss together over the spring semester. Karen will register in her first graduate-level course at the Hometown University, the summer course K535 Collaboration and Co-Teaching. Donnie will develop his first-year professional growth plan and gain his principal's approval. His plan includes making three trips to Down the Road High School to observe the teacher of the year, nationally recognized for quality inclusive

practices and co-teaching expertise. We are enthused with the possibilities and realize the imperative to prioritize and complete appropriate conversations from the value-added critical conversations framework.

- **Not-so-smart goal statement**—We will work to improve the health and fitness of our students.

- **SMARTER goal statement**—By November 15, 2015, our school will eliminate all marketing of foods and beverages not meeting our nutrition standards, and offer appealing and nutritious alternatives during the school day and at afterschool events and activities—especially those that are attended mainly by students as an extension of the school day.

- **Not-so-smart goal statement**—All of our students will achieve up to their potential.

- **SMARTER goal statement**—We will increase the percentage of students in our Hometown School co-taught class who are on track to catch up to proficiency in reading from 33 percent in 2011 to 40 percent in 2012, as measured by the Almighty State Growth Model, using more appropriate and engaging materials and instruction.

- **Not-so-smart goal statement**—We will improve the students who really need it.

- **Not-so-smart goal statement**—We will work to help those students with special needs to prepare for testing.

- **SMARTER goal statement**—We will decrease the gap in the percent proficient among students eligible for free- or reduced-price lunch and those who are not from 20 percentage points in 2011 to 10 percentage points in 2023. The reduction in the gap will be a result of increased proficiency of students eligible for free- or reduced-price lunch, and not a decrease in the percent proficient for those that are not eligible.

Now write your own collaborative SMARTER goals.

SPECIAL OCCASION CONVERSATIONS

Asking Our Families—*Assessing Protocol*

Just how friendly is your co-teaching environment for your students and their families? We don't have to look far to find ample research on just how important it is to include families in our schools and classrooms. Hopefully your school district provides a welcoming environment for all of your students and their families. You and your partner can go a long way toward ensuring that families do feel comfortable by talking about the ways that you already invite family members to participate more fully in their children's learning experiences. You can also explore the challenges that families might have in taking part so that together you can design helpful strategies that will increase the likelihood that you and your families are true collaborative partners.

Together with your partner, answer the following questions about family engagement. Use your responses to help recruit more families to join in your efforts and strengthen existing relationships.

- What signs in our classroom and in the school environment give a welcoming message to our students' families?

- Are these signs accessible and meaningful to all of our students' families?

- How do families learn about our co-teaching efforts, why this practice will benefit their students, and how they can help?

- When and how do we invite in and communicate with our students' families?

- When and how do we engage our students' families in learning and social activities?

- Are there time, travel, language, cultural, and childcare issues we could address to make involvement less difficult?

- What other barriers might our students' families have that could be limiting their participation?

- Are we willing to make home visits or to provide language and other accessibility supports?

- Might we identify and use bridges—school allies who already have access to communities we might not have access to currently?

- Are there benefits we might offer our students' families to encourage their active participation? In what ways might we ask them what benefits they would like to have available?

Brainstorm with your partner all of the ways you might show your collaborative strength by working together to increase engagement with the families of your students.

Having a World Café for Student Voices—*Assessing Protocol*

The World Café movement (Brown & Isaacs, 2005) invites us to enter into a conversational process that is based on a set of design principles, hosting conversations about questions that matter. The movement supports the concept that collectively we have access to all the wisdom and resources we need. It asks us to consider some what ifs:

- What if the future is born of webs of human conversation?

- What if compelling questions encourage collective learning?

- What if networks are the underlying pattern of living systems?

- What if intelligence emerges as the system connects to itself in diverse and creative ways?

With your partner, share your thoughts on these premises presented by World Café. Do you agree? What do you question? What do you dispute?

If you are open to a new way to hear from your students, plan and conduct a World Café in the classes that you co-teach. Use the following principles as you plan your event:

- Narrow the focus. Perhaps you will want to focus on community building in your classroom or your co-teaching efforts.

- Create a hospitable space.

- Explore questions that matter. They should matter to you, but especially to your students.

- Connect diverse perspectives. Encourage free thoughts and open dialogue.

- Encourage each student's contributions. Work to ensure that everyone participates.

- Listen together for patterns, insights, and deeper questions.

- Share collective discoveries. Debrief the process with your students. Afterward, debrief as facilitators.

You can plan this activity like a town meeting, or create stations with topics of interest in order to engage your students. This will allow you not only to hear one another, but to help inform decisions about how you refine your learning environment and differentiate your teaching delivery and student performance and product choices.

Setting Professional and Personal Goals—*Goal-Setting Protocol*

With your co-teacher choose one personal goal, one individual professional goal, and one or two professional-partnership or team goals to focus on as priorities for improvement for the coming school year.

For each goal, develop at least three strategies or action steps that will likely lead to improvement. State the specific actions you will take to build better skills. Also, set a date by which you will have begun the steps.

Finally, consider what type of support you may need to sustain the improvement goals or continue to make progress toward your goals. Use figure 7.5 to guide you through these steps.

Figure 7.5: Professional and personal goals.

Goal	Strategies/Action Steps	By When?	How to Sustain?
Personal goal			
Individual professional goal			
Partner or team goal			
Partner or team goal			

*Visit **go.solution-tree.com/specialneeds** to download and print this figure.*

Prioritizing Our Co-Teaching Characteristics—*Planning Protocol*

Individually, list at least ten of the most important collaboration characteristics that you believe to be key elements of a successful co-teaching partnership.

Compare lists with your co-teaching partner or your team.

With your co-teaching partner or team, come to a consensus on the top five elements, and write them in the left column of figure 7.6 on page 114. For each partnership or team you participate in, you may have a different top-five list, so you will want to fill out a separate protocol for each of those groups. It might be helpful to write a few success indicators below each characteristic to show just what you mean by citing each of them.

Check the column on the continuum that best demonstrates your progress on each of the characteristics.

Finally, because you have agreed that these are the most important characteristics, discuss with your partners how you might improve each of these characteristics. If you have achieved good marks in the characteristics you listed as your top five, then go on to the next group of characteristics that you deem important.

Figure 7.6: Our co-teaching characteristics progress assessment.

Co-Teaching Characteristics	Just Getting Started	Emerging	Midway There	Pretty Good	Advanced

Visit **go.solution-tree.com/specialneeds** to download and print this figure.

Examples of effective co-teaching characteristics might include such things as:

- Shared vision
- Shared resources
- Effective working relationship
- Effective and open communication
- Effective planning
- Flexibility
- Parity
- Collaborative environment
- Understanding of learner development
- Understanding of learning differences
- Content knowledge and expertise
- Innovative applications of content
- Assessment process
- Good planning process
- Variety of instructional strategies and co-teaching models
- Reflection practitioner skills
- Openness
- Desire for continuous growth
- Processes for planning, decision making, problem solving
- Understanding and commitment to meeting professional standards where appropriate
- Understanding and commitment to align with district, local, state initiatives where appropriate
- Solid work ethic

Asking Twenty Questions — *Planning Protocol*

With your partner, come to a consensus on the questions in the assessment Twenty Questions: How Inclusive Are You? (fig. 7.7). These guiding questions are divided into three sections: (1) students, (2) adults, and (3) professional practice. Your discussions around these questions will help paint a picture of the frame of mind of you're setting when it comes to inclusive practices for all students. You might want to begin with assessing your partnership, and later expand to the entire faculty.

This activity actually came to us while working with an elementary school whose principal had called us to help his faculty become more collaborative. We opened our first town meeting with the teachers with a guiding question about the climate as they began the school year. We were informed that the teachers had spent the entire previous summer working to ensure that major emphasis was placed on the development of character education. In fact, respect was the schoolwide theme for the year, and the school was covered with messages relating to respect. It didn't take long for the teachers to let us know all they were doing to "get their students to start respecting them and one another," and yet something didn't seem right to us.

It wasn't clear until the lone male, a second-year teacher in the building, shared his observation of the faculty. He said that while the students did seem to be responding to the "respect" strategies, the teachers were not being held to the same standards. After gasps of incredulity, he continued. He said he felt, in fact, that the teachers were actually quite mean to one another, cliques were commonplace, and the teachers' lounge should actually be deemed toxic and off limits. Every morning he watched as several teachers walked right past him without even speaking, let alone giving a pleasant good morning greeting. He had heard everyone praise how inclusive they had become by learning about character education, but their day-to-day practice failed to demonstrate that it was more than a script to be used during the fifteen minutes allotted to the curriculum twice a week.

We adapted the twenty questions to help begin conversations so schools could determine just how operational their inclusive practices are on a daily basis. Using these questions has been a real eye-opener for many schools whose members believed that they were inclusive. Other schools have successfully followed up with the Consensogram protocol on page 119. Both of these protocols might help prompt your faculty to come up with evidence to prove or disprove their initial responses to the issues raised.

Figure 7.7: Twenty questions: How inclusive are you?

	What We Believe	What the Evidence Suggests	Our Plan to Address the Discrepancies
Students			
1. Are students with and without disabilities considered full members of the school community?			
2. Does the school climate promote membership and respect for all students?			

continued →

Special Occasion Conversations

	What We Believe	What the Evidence Suggests	Our Plan to Address the Discrepancies
Students			
3. Do students have opportunities to develop and enhance meaningful social relationships?			
4. Do all students receive services based on their individual needs, including transition needs and community access?			
5. Are students and their families effective members of the educational team?			
6. Do students and their families have a designated role in achieving their educational outcomes?			
Adults			
7. Do leaders support collaboration and inclusion through policies, procedures, and practices?			
8. Do job descriptions for special educators, general educators, and paraeducators address all students and emphasize collaborative teaching?			
9. Do special and general education administrators share teacher supervision and evaluation responsibilities?			
10. Do school leaders support professional learning communities and ongoing, comprehensive professional development?			
11. Are all teachers considered full members of the school faculty?			
Adults			
12. Do teachers use common planning time effectively for collaboration and co-teaching?			
13. Do teachers solve learning challenges and make decisions as a team rather than in isolation?			

	What We Believe	What the Evidence Suggests	Our Plan to Address the Discrepancies
Adults			
14. Do teams incorporate co-teaching models on a regular basis?			
15. Is the IEP program understood, developed, and implemented using a collaborative team process to best support students?			
Professional Practice			
16. Is the general education curriculum used as the basis for all student instruction?			
17. Do teachers know and use research-based best practices for teaching and learning in their work with all students?			
18. Does the faculty jointly discuss and make decisions about curriculum, instruction, grading, evaluation, and assessment issues?			
19. Are a variety of evaluation and assessment strategies utilized to evaluate instruction and learning and to guide all students in self-assessment?			
20. Are relevant curriculum and instructional supports (including adaptations and modifications) natural considerations of teaching practice, in order to prepare students for future home, work, learning, and recreational environments?			

*Adapted with permission from Cole, Horvath, Sprague, Wilcox & Pratt, 1999. Copyright Indiana Institute on Disability and Community, Indiana University. Visit **go.solution-tree.com/specialneeds** to download and print this figure.*

IN A PERFECT WORLD CONVERSATIONS

Talking About Responsibility—*Assessing Protocol*

Robert Starratt's ethical leadership model (2004) offers relevant questions as we ponder our partnerships. We might ask one another the following questions:

How are we responsible *to* . . .

- Students, teachers, administrators, and staff
- Families, school district officials
- National, state, and local governing agencies

How are we responsible *for* . . .

- Creating and sustaining authentic collaborative relationships with all partners and stakeholders
- Creating and sustaining a healthy learning environment
- The teaching and learning of all students

How are we responsible *as* . . .

- Human beings
- Educators
- Citizens

Consider for a moment who we are responsible *to*, who we are responsible *for*, and who we are responsible *as*. With your partner, brainstorm the responsibilities for each area Starratt points to in his work. Use the following questions to help guide your conversations about responsibility.

- How can we use our view of the future to frame a conversation about shared vision?
- What are the values and beliefs we share?
- What are we learning about one another?
- How might we blend the values and beliefs we each bring to this relationship?

Using Metaphors and Models That Engage Students—
Planning Protocol

A creative team of young teachers took the station model to new heights with their "medical model." An elementary reading specialist, a fifth-grade teacher, a sixth-grade teacher, and a speech communications specialist decided to replicate a hospital setting during a recent environmental unit culminating in teams of students developing research projects on approved environmental topics. They used a variety of models to present the material, but soon realized that because the students had not been in co-teaching classrooms before, they needed to be taught how to work effectively in cooperative groups. When the students gained the necessary preparation, they were given daily group time for the week to write their research paper assignments.

The medical model translated easily for the students: if they needed additional support or felt they were in trouble, they worked with teachers who were manning the emergency room. If they were able to work fairly independently, they were in the general operating room. When students were ready for peer editing, they went to the surgery wing. From surgery, they could choose to have the appropriate therapy, either in rooms for reconstruction or to the enhancement therapy group.

Given the appropriate preparation, this model might work beautifully as a way to differentiate instruction and provide support by engaging *all* students creatively. The model also has the possibility

In a Perfect World Conversation

of fostering self-advocacy as students were responsible for analyzing their team's needs and finding the appropriate resources.

The example metaphor gives you a quick idea of how these particular co-teaching partners viewed and described their relationship and how they worked together and with their students. Keeping that in mind, follow the steps below as you and your partners consider your own co-teaching practice.

1 Review your co-teaching experiences with your partner. This will serve as the basis for this protocol.

2 With your partner, decide on a metaphor that you could use to compare to your co-teaching experience: Our collaboration is like _____ because _____. (List three to five reasons why.)

3 Explain how these three to five characteristics of your metaphor are similar to your collaboration.

Many partners have found that this is a great way to introduce co-teaching with other faculty members. Add some excitement by actually using materials and props to illustrate your metaphors.

Getting to Consensus: A Consensogram—*Assessing Protocol*

In order to develop a collaborative, inclusive frame of mind with your partner and all of your colleagues, you may also want to consider how you fare on the consensogram. This instrument is most effective when you mark your comments individually and then discuss them with your partner or other colleagues. Sometimes just checking on our individual perceptions leads to informative and enriching conversations that help us develop and strengthen our frame of mind when it comes to inclusive practices. As you make your marks, be sure to cite evidence that leads you to your decisions and challenge one another with not only the evidence, but how we interpret it.

Once you come to an agreement on the state of inclusive practice in your setting, discuss how you will ensure that you are supporting all students in every way that you can.

Consider each of the focus areas in figure 7.8 (page 120), and mark the boxes that best reflect your own understanding of how inclusive your school is. Use this assessment to help steer conversations with colleagues to a more inclusive environment for all students.

In a Perfect World Conversations

In a Perfect World Conversation

Figure 7.8: Consensogram for inclusive school communities.

Focus	Ideal	Not There Yet	Emerging	Inclusive	Evidence
Inclusion	We are an inclusive school community.	We do not engage in discussions pertaining to full membership of all students.	We talk about inclusion, but the actual practice is limited.	We purposefully consider how to best include all students in instruction and activities.	
Collaborative community	We are a collaborative learning community.	We typically work in isolation or with a single partner.	We share full responsibility for inclusive schools as a goal.	We effectively share responsibility for and commitment to ourselves as learners.	

Focus	Ideal	Not There Yet	Emerging	Inclusive	Evidence
Elements of inclusive schools	We can identify the rationale, purpose, and characteristics of inclusive school communities.	We discuss segments of our school population in isolation (students at risk, students from different cultures).	We have begun to consider the purpose for inclusive school communities as it applies to all students and staff.	We have a shared definition, rationale, and purpose of our inclusive school community.	
Change process	We have examined the factors that influence, impede, and facilitate school change.	We tend to avoid discussions that may cause conflict.	We have begun to consider the factors that influence decisions and school change.	We actively seek, examine, and honestly discuss factors that influence school change.	
Using data to inform decisions	We collect and use data to identify issues and inform our decision making.	We do not use data to inform us.	We have begun to collect data and are learning how to use them to support student success.	We use data to drive our decisions concerning professional development, curriculum, instruction, and school structure.	
Designing and implementing inclusive schools	We design a framework for the development and implementation of an inclusive school plan.	We have not considered a framework and are overwhelmed by the prospect.	We recognize the need for a framework and have begun preliminary discussions.	We have a shared vision of the framework and will actively and collaboratively work toward design implementation.	

Visit go.solution-tree.com/specialneeds to download and print this figure.

CRITICAL CONVERSATIONS PROTOCOLS: SET 3— ENHANCE INSTRUCTION

8

This chapter contains the detailed conversations protocols for set 3, Enhance Instruction. These step-by-step activities will help you and your partner or team develop more effective co-teaching practice. The chapter begins with focus questions and anticipated outcomes and contains three types of conversations: (1) non-negotiable, (2) special occasion, and (3) in a perfect world.

The focus questions will give you an idea of what you'll learn in this set of protocols. The outcomes provide measures to help you determine if you and your partner have covered the kinds of conversations that will help you be successful when you move to the next set. The Reflective Journal (page 46) will help you monitor your progress through the series of protocols.

Visit **go.solution-tree.com/specialneeds** to download the reproducibles for this chapter.

Focus Questions

- How will we employ co-teaching models that are matched to the instructional needs of our students?
- How will we use co-teaching models to align our instructional content with standards, curriculum goals, and assessment?
- How can we incorporate evidence-based practices into our co-teaching efforts?
- How do we align our practice with professional standards and other district initiatives such as differentiated instruction (DI), universal design for learning (UDL), professional learning communities (PLCs), response to intervention (RTI), and so on?

> **Anticipated Outcomes**
>
> - We understand and are able to use a variety of co-teaching models based on the instructional needs of our students.
> - Our co-teaching practice matches co-teaching models to our instructional content (with standards, curriculum goals, and assessment).
> - We incorporate evidenced-based practices into our co-teaching efforts.
> - We align our practice with professional standards and other district initiatives, such as differentiated instruction (DI), universal design for learning (UDL), professional learning communities (PLCs), response to intervention (RTI), and so on.

NON-NEGOTIABLE CONVERSATIONS

Adding Value With Co-Teaching—*Planning Protocol*

This protocol will help you determine when to use the specific co-teaching models in your shared practice (see chapter 2, Co-Teaching Models, for specific information about the different models).

Using figure 8.1, with your partner, discuss the strengths and challenges of each of the models. Determine how implementing the model will yield a greater return on investment than if just one of you were teaching the same content. Remember this is just a starting point as you begin to build your own repertoire of models using these examples.

As you implement the models, be sure to make notes about what worked, what could be improved another time, and what additional collaborators might be included to support your efforts with the implementation. Begin to build your own repertoire of models using these examples.

Figure 8.1: Co-teaching model assessment.

Co-Teaching Models	Strengths	Challenges	Value Added	Our Applications
Complementary—One teaches, one observes and supports the other teacher				
Complementary—One teaches, one observes and supports students				
Side by side—Alternative grouping				
Side by side—Parallel grouping				
Side by side—Station/learning-center grouping				

Co-Teaching Models	Strengths	Challenges	Value Added	Our Applications
Teaming				
Our variations				

*Visit **go.solution-tree.com/specialneeds** to download and print this figure.*

Value-Added Co-Teaching—*Planning Protocol*

How can we plan our co-teaching lessons, units, or activities to ensure that each of us is underpromising and overdelivering? How can we be sure that families and administrators will see the return on investment that we are offering students?

Effective co-teachers are in the habit of incorporating the information in the Value-Added Co-Teaching Planning Form (fig. 8.2) into their instructional planning format. This specificity helps ensure that each of the partners has active roles and responsibilities. Use the form to plan with your partner so that you know explicitly how to divide the labor and how you will each be actively engaged in purposeful work throughout your class times.

Figure 8.2: Value-added co-teaching planning form.

Co-teachers: Shared Class/Subject(s):   Today's Planning Date:

Teaching Session No.:   Day(s): Mon. Tues. Wed. Thurs. Fri.

Lesson plan will be used during the week(s) of:

Next Planning Session:

Day: Time: Location: Date:

Learning Outcomes
1.
2.
3.
4.
5.

Date	What Will the Co-Teachers Be Doing? (Activity, Format, and Content)	What Will the Students Be Doing?	Accommodation Strategies	Evaluation Strategies
	1. 2. 3.			

*Adapted from Gable, Hendrickson, Evans, Frye, & Bryant, 1993, p. 19. Visit **go.solution-tree.com /specialneeds** to download and print this figure.*

Figure 8.3: Co-teaching alignment planning template 1.

Grade:	Related Standards:	Learning Opportunities:	Authentic Assessments:	Tools, Materials, Resources Needed:
Subject:			Planned Outcomes:	
	Underlying Knowledge and Skills:	Instructional Opportunities:		
Number of Students:			Academic Outcomes:	
Project:	Academic, Social, Community Impact:		Personal/Social Development Outcomes:	
Lesson Objectives:			Civic Responsibility Outcomes:	
			Career Outcomes:	

Engagement: How will students be engaged in age-appropriate decision-making processes during this project?

Student Reflection: What ongoing reflection techniques will be used to allow students to connect their service efforts to the larger reality around them?

Shared/Individual Responsibilities:

Estimated Project Length:
Roles/Shared Responsibilities With Timeline:

August	September	October	November	December	January	February	March	April	May	June/July

Alignment With Other School Initiatives:

Lessons Learned Upon Completion of Project—What worked? What could be improved?

Visit go.solution-tree.com/specialneeds to download and print this figure.

Co-Teaching Alignment— *Planning Protocol*

While you and your partner will eventually revise or design your own co-teaching planning templates, it is helpful to consider some of the ways other partners have decided to plan together. In addition to the planning template found in the previous protocol, we offer two additional versions for you to consider. See the reproducible Co-Teaching Alignment Planning Template 1 (fig. 8.3) and Template 2 (fig. 8.4).

Figure 8.4: Co-teaching alignment planning template 2.

Co-teachers		Class		
Lesson, Unit, or Activity (Circle one and list the title.)	**Collaboration topics: What tasks will we have to do to implement the plan?**	**Who will do each task?**	**When will the task be completed?**	**How will we measure our success? Outcome? Product?**
Lesson: Unit: Activity:				
Lesson: Unit: Activity:				

*Visit **go.solution-tree.com/specialneeds** to download and print this figure.*

Having an Accountability Chat— *Reflecting Protocol*

Now that we have solid plans about how to plan for and implement quality designs for learning that match our students, our teaching, and our practice, how can we be sure that we are measuring up? Would others see us as accountable, as responsible professionals?

Sometimes we feel we are on the right track, but with just a little bit of feedback we can show vast improvements. For instance, the piano tuner listens to the notes then tweaks the instrument, sometimes in huge ways, but often with subtle measures, making the notes better, clearer, and in tune with the others on the keyboard.

As partners, select a specific aspect of your teaching, planning, or assessment on which you want feedback. Then invite a few trusted colleagues to provide helpful feedback using an accountability chat. Be sure to hand out the Accountability Chat Form (fig. 8.5, page 126) to each participant before beginning so they can record their feedback and take notes. Use the following steps to conduct these chats in the most meaningful and efficient way:

1 Individually decide on a plan, delivery, dilemma, or other issue or situation for which you would like to become more accountable. Then present that situation to your partner. Try to be concise and limit your presentation to approximately four minutes.

2 Give your partner a chance to ask clarifying questions.

3 Ask your partner to reflect on what he or she heard, and respond as if you aren't present. Be sure there is *not* an exchange during this time.

4   Then ask your partner to provide warm feedback, offering specific ideas he or she liked and positive notes about your presentation, for approximately four minutes.

5   Next, ask your partner to offer cool feedback designed to help give suggestions for improvement, ways that the collaboration and co-teaching might change, or how to adjust activities to become more efficient and effective.

6   Finally, respond to the feedback you heard.

You might also use this protocol to expand and improve your collaborative practice when you're faced with a challenge or when you want to try a new strategy.

Figure 8.5: Accountability chat form.

Notes	Clarifying Questions
Warm Feedback	Cool Feedback
Reflections for Improvement and Refining	

Visit **go.solution-tree.com/specialneeds** *to download and print this figure.*

SPECIAL OCCASION CONVERSATIONS

Aligning With Evidence-Based Practices—*Assessing Protocol*

How do we know what changes to make to move theory into practice? What evidence or research-based practices should we be incorporating? How can we tell which experts to pay attention to? This activity will help you sift through the research and use what is most valuable depending on your students and your situation.

Begin the activity by using figure 8.6 individually to estimate how much you and your partner (or school as a whole) currently know, understand, and do to incorporate research-based practices into your classroom. Then complete the remainder of the chart with your co-teacher.

You may begin by prioritizing your top choices by deciding which evidence-based topics are the most meaningful and relevant for your collaborative practice. It will be helpful as a baseline to learn which areas are being addressed well and which areas need more attention as you begin to make changes in your practices.

Figure 8.6: Aligning theories to collaborative practice activity.

Evidence-Based Topics	Our Understanding of the Research	What the Research Says	What Our Practice Shows We Do	How We Might Use Our Collaborative Practice to Maximize This Research-Based Topic
Brain research				
Literacy, reading, math				
Leadership				
Demographics				
Differentiation				
Expectations				
Professional development				
Student engagement				
Instructional matching				
Positive behavior supports				
Cultural competence				
Other evidence-based practices that are relevant to your district				

*Visit **go.solution-tree.com/specialneeds** to download and print this figure.*

Aligning With Differentiated Instruction (DI)—*Aligning Protocol*

Consider how the following principles of differentiated instruction (Tomlinson & McTighe, 2006) might apply to your co-teaching practices. These key features of differentiated instruction provide a way in which to situate your own planning, instruction, and assessment of the student learning process:

1 Good teaching is predicated upon a teacher's clarity about what a learner should know, understand, and be able to do as a result of a given learning experience and set of learning experiences.

2 All learners focus much of their time and attention on the key concepts, principles, and skills identified by the teacher as essential to growth and development in the subject—but

at varying degrees of abstractness, complexity, open-endedness, problem clarity, and structure.

3 All learners should work with "respectful tasks"—those tasks that recognize each student's ability to do quality, yet differentiated work.

4 All learners are provided different routes to content, activities, and products in response to differing learner needs.

5 Flexible grouping of students enables all learners to work in a wide variety of configurations and with a full range of peers, while targeting specific learning needs.

As you discuss these principles with your co-teaching partner, how might you reconceptualize your joint practice to ensure that you—as individuals and as a teaching partnership—continually consider these key concepts within your own planning and implementation?

Aligning With Universal Design for Differentiated Instruction (UDDI)— *Planning Protocol*

In today's schools, the mix of students is more diverse than ever. Educators are challenged to teach all kinds of learners to high standards, yet a single classroom may include students who struggle to learn for any number of reasons, such as the following:

- Learning disabilities
- English language barriers
- Emotional or behavioral problems
- Lack of interest or engagement
- Sensory and physical disabilities

Teachers want their students to succeed, but a one-size-fits-all approach to education simply does not work. How can teachers respond to individual differences?

The Understanding by Design (UbD) framework developed by Wiggins and McTighe (2005) helps teachers apply the principles of Differentiated Instruction (Tomlinson, 2001) to ensure that all students succeed in meaningful, appropriately challenging learning experiences. Adding the principles of Universal Design for Learning (UDL; Rose & Meyer, 2002) encourages professional educators to consider and plan to reduce barriers to access and to provide multiple means of representation, expression, and engagement for all learners. These principles have effectively been combined into Universal Design for Differentiated Instruction (UDDI). This powerful framework provides educators with knowledge to enhance skills in designing rigorous units of study that respect learner differences.

UDDI calls for *multiple means of representation*, to give learners various ways of acquiring information and knowledge; *multiple means of action and expression*, to provide learners with alternatives for demonstrating what they know; and *multiple means of engagement*, to tap into learners' interests, offer appropriate challenges, and increase motivation.

Curriculum is defined broadly to include four basic components:

1 Goals and Desired Outcomes—The benchmarks or expectations for teaching and learning often made explicit in the form of a scope and sequence of skills to be addressed

> 2 **Assessment**—The reasons for and methods of measuring student progress including summative, formative, and preassessment explicitly aligned with specified outcomes
>
> 3 **Methods**—The planned learning experiences that are differentiated to encourage active engagement, shared learning, and real-world application
>
> 4 **Materials**—The technology, media, and tools used for teaching and learning

The term *curriculum* is often used to describe only the goals, objectives, or plans, something distinct from the "means" of methods, materials, and assessment. Yet since each of these components is essential for effective learning—and since each includes hidden barriers that undermine student efforts to become master learners—curriculum design should consider each of them as a piece.

These guidelines apply to the general education curriculum, which, when universally designed, should meet the educational needs of most students, including those with disabilities. Consideration of this UDDI planning protocol can help guide the design of expectations, content, methods, and outcomes across differing classrooms in each school or system.

Discuss how incorporating the principles of UDDI will assist you in your collaborative work. What evidence do you have that your district is moving to a UDDI plan? Are there sufficient supports to move this concept along? How might you use your collaborative work to further the concept of UDDI?

During your co-teaching planning time, review the framework for UDDI. How might you incorporate this format and the principles of UDDI to assist you in adding value to your co-teaching practice? Take a look at the basic concepts of UDDI as presented in the left-hand column of figure 8.7. By using the UDDI components and talking through these with your co-teaching partner, you will find key ways to complement the planning, instruction, and assessment for your students. Your descriptions in each area should also include how each partner carries out the parts and how the partnership works together to implement the plan fully.

Responding to Response to Intervention (RTI) — *Planning Protocol*

In this conversation you and your partner will explore, select, and adapt a variety of co-teaching models as appropriate by considering your teaching partner, your students, and your curriculum and instruction using the principles of RTI.

RTI is the practice of (1) providing high-quality instruction and intervention matched to student needs and (2) using learning rates over time and levels of performance to (3) make important educational decisions. These three components of RTI are essential.

Figure 8.7: Aligning with UDDI: A planning framework.

Stage 1—desired results:	
Understanding: Students will understand that . . .	Essential questions:
Students will know . . . (vocabulary terms, the story, actual information about a topic, and so on)	Students will be able to . . .

continued →

Special Occasion Conversations

Stage 2—assessment evidence:	
Performance task(s):	Other evidence:

Stage 3—learning plan:	
Learning activities:	Accommodations:

Stage 1	Stage 2	Stage 3
If the desired result is for the learners to . . .	Then you need evidence of the student's ability to . . .	Then the learning activities need to . . .
Understand that: And thoughtfully consider the question(s):	Then the assessment needs to include some things like . . .	Help students to . . . by . . .

Source: From Understanding by Design: Professional Development Workbook *(p. 31) by Grant Wiggins & Jay McTighe, Alexandria, VA: ASCD. © 2004 by ASCD. Reprinted and adapted with permission. Learn more about ASCD at www.ascd.org.*

In RTI, high-quality instruction and intervention are matched to student need, demonstrated through scientific research and practice to produce high learning rates for most students. Educators assess students' individual responses and make modifications to instruction and intervention goals depending on the results.

Learning rate and level of performance are the primary sources of information used in ongoing decision making. These refer to a student's growth in achievement or behavior competencies over time compared to prior levels of performance and peer growth levels.

Important educational decisions about intensity and likely duration of interventions are based on individual student response to instruction across three tiers of instruction and intervention. Decisions about the necessity of more intense interventions, including eligibility for special education, come from special education or other services.

Discuss how the considerations and implementation of RTI, adapted from the National Association of State Directors of Special Education (2008) and the National Research Center on Learning Disabilities (NRCLD; 2005), in figure 8.8 might affect or support your collaborative practice.

Inviting Marzano Into Our Conversations — *Planning Protocol*

Robert Marzano (2003) has synthesized thirty years of research to provide clear insight into the nature of schooling. He defines factors affecting student achievement by offering the following questions:

- How can schools set academic goals that do not underestimate student potential?

Figure 8.8: Responding to response to intervention elements, guiding questions, and implementation ideas.

RTI Elements	Guiding Questions	Implementation Ideas
1. High-quality instruction and intervention are matched to student need, demonstrated through scientific research and practice to produce high learning rates for most students. Individual responses are assessed and modifications to instruction and intervention goals are made depending on results with individual students.	How might we use co-teaching to provide high-quality instruction and intervention for all of our students?	
2. Learning rate and level of performance are the primary sources of information used in ongoing decision making. These refer to a student's growth in achievement or behavior competencies over time compared to prior levels of performance and peer-growth levels.	How can our collaborative practice support our desired learning rate and level of performance goals?	
3. Important educational decisions—about intensity and likely duration of interventions—are based on individual student response to instruction across multiple tiers of interventions. Decisions about the necessity of more intense interventions, including eligibility for special education, come from special education or other services.	How can we collaborate to ensure that educational decisions are based on individual responses across multiple tiers of intervention?	
4. A three-tier model of school supports provides academic and behavioral system supports: Tier 1—Core instruction for all students Tier 2—Targeted group interventions Tier 3—Intense, individual interventions	Discuss with your partner how you might use the three tiers of support in your collaborative practice.	

*Source: National Association of State Directors of Special Education, 2008, p. 3, and NRCLD, 2005. Visit **go.solution-tree.com/specialneeds** to download and print this figure.*

- How critical are staff collegiality and professional development?
- Do all students have equal opportunity to learn, given current curriculum requirements?
- Supplemental versus required content—is there room for redefinition?
- What types of parental and community involvement make a real difference?
- What instructional strategies really work?
- What influence can an individual teacher have on students?
- How can teachers manage classrooms that promote positive student/teacher relationships?
- How can teachers structure their curricula to better sequence and pace content?

Special Occasion Conversations

- Can teachers really overcome a student's negative home environment?

- How does an understanding of motivation theories help students and teachers overcome learning obstacles?

- What specific learning strategies can enhance learned intelligence and background knowledge?

Marzano (2003) recommends specific action steps to implement successful strategies culled from the wealth of research data. Discuss with your partner how value-added co-teaching might allow you to incorporate Marzano's instructional best practices. They include:

- Identifying similarities and differences

- Summarizing and note-taking

- Using homework and practice-feedback

- Using nonlinguistic representations

- Using cooperative learning

- Setting objectives and feedback

- Generating and testing a hypothesis

- Using cues, questions, and advanced organizers

Considering Cultural Competence—*Aligning Protocol*

Each month, Sarah W. Nelson and Patricia L. Guerra write a column in Learning Forward's *JSD* about the importance of and strategies for developing cultural awareness in teachers and schools. We especially like the four-stage model for developing cultural proficiency that they have created (Nelson & Guerra, 2011, p. 56). They stress that this concept of cultural competence is very dynamic, based on a notion of continuous growth.

Their four-stage model for developing cultural proficiency suggests the following components.

Stage 1: Raise the issue—Through examination of all kinds of student data, educators see that a lack of cultural proficiency impacts student learning opportunities.

Stage 2: Assess readiness—Those leading professional learning communities conduct simulations and assessments to determine learners' readiness to engage in cultural proficiency work and differentiate learning accordingly.

Stage 3: Increase knowledge of cultural variation and surface deficit beliefs—A variety of learning options encourages learners to investigate their own culture and its influence on teaching and to explore the cultural backgrounds of students and community members.

Stage 4: Challenge and reframe deficient beliefs—In this stage, teachers have opportunities to explore and discuss their beliefs and practices, with facilitators helping them shift their thinking and actions to create equitable learning for all students.

With your partner, complete the following template (fig. 8.9) to help you better understand your own cultural proficiency. Think of this from a personal standpoint, but also how your collective responses affect the choices you make as you plan and teach together. The information you glean from doing this will hopefully inform your understanding of your students and their families. These cultural understandings will allow you to be much more effective at designing instructional strategies that ensure the success of students who have different life experiences from your own.

Figure 8.9: Stages of cultural proficiency template.

Stage of Cultural Proficiency	Evidence We Already Do This	Proactive Steps to Help Us Be More Culturally Proficient
Stage 1 **Raise the issue**—Through examination of all kinds of student data, educators see that a lack of cultural proficiency impacts student learning opportunities.		
Stage 2 **Assess readiness**—Those leading professional learning communities conduct simulations and assessments to determine learners' readiness to engage in cultural proficiency work and differentiate learning accordingly.		
Stage 3 **Increase knowledge of cultural variation and surface deficit beliefs**—A variety of learning options encourages learners to investigate their own culture and its influence on teaching and to explore the cultural backgrounds of students and community members.		
Stage 4 **Challenge and reframe deficient beliefs**—In this stage, teachers have opportunities to explore and discuss their beliefs and practices, with facilitators helping them shift their thinking and actions to create equitable learning for all students.		

Source: Nelson & Guerra, 2011, p. 56. Visit **go.solution-tree.com/specialneeds** *to download and print this figure.*

Aligning With Global Competence—*Aligning Protocol*

As we plan our collaborative lessons, we are constantly aware of what we are doing in our classrooms to prepare our students for the global economy. The Asia Society (2008, p. 12) has prepared a list of ten questions for you to ask your school or community as you become more intentional in fostering global competence in the 21st century (fig. 8.10, page 134). Each of these questions can serve as a prompt for schoolwide conversations. Keeping in mind that the value of co-teaching is that it allows us to improve our instruction to meet student needs, global competence is certainly a necessary consideration. The questions are also worth considering as you and your partner plan your collaborative instruction. Remain open-minded as you consider these questions.

The Council of Chief State School Officers' EdSteps Project (2010), in partnership with Asia Society, also identifies four components of global competence in their Global Competence Matrix: (1) Investigating the world, when students explore the world beyond their own immediate environments, (2) recognizing perspectives, when students can see their own perspectives and the perspectives of others, (3) communicating ideas, when students exchange ideas with diverse audiences in effective ways,

Special Occasion Conversations

and (4) taking action, when students transform their ideas and findings into actions to improve the world around them. Consider with your copartner or collaborative teams, or with your entire faculty, ways to address and build global competence in your students. Begin with the following questions (NSDC, 2010):

- How do our students investigate the world in our classrooms through our curriculum and lessons? What global issues or challenges could we add to our collaboratively taught lessons to help students explore the world more deeply?

- What opportunities do we give our students to experience and consider perspectives from others, and how do we encourage them to reflect on and discover their own perspectives?

- How do our students communicate their ideas with diverse audiences? Do they have opportunities to communicate with other students from around the world?

- How do our students take action and impact the world through service to their local or global community?

Figure 8.10: Global competence questions.

Questions	Implications for Your Collaborative Practice
1. What are your state and local connections to other parts of the world, including economic development, cultural exchanges, and population diversity?	
2. What knowledge, skills, and values do graduates need to function effectively in the interconnected world of the 21st century?	
3. How might your school's curriculum be strengthened to promote international knowledge and skills?	
4. What is the status of world language study, including less commonly taught languages?	
5. How can technology resources be used to extend the international knowledge and experience of teachers and students?	
6. What kinds of international exchange programs for students and educators are now available or should be?	
7. What international expertise do your teachers or administrators have, and what professional development opportunities exist or can be developed to help them to gain more?	
8. Which local ethnic communities or language groups can be tapped to strengthen learning about the world? Which partnerships can be created with colleges, businesses, and cultural or international affairs organizations to help enhance students' and teachers' international knowledge?	
9. What student leadership opportunities or community service activities exist or could be developed to promote students' democratic values, citizenship, and global understanding?	
10. How can your school and community libraries, after-school programs, and other informal learning resources be used to promote learning about the world?	

*Source: Asia Society, 2008, p. 12. Visit **go.solution-tree.com/specialneeds** to download and print this figure.*

Now, with your partner, design collaborative units of study or individual lessons to help your students master the knowledge, skills, and dispositions to understand and act creatively and innovatively on issues of global significance (fig. 8.11).

Figure 8.11: Major components of global competence.

Global Competence Components	Instructional Strategies for Our Collaborative Partnership
Investigate the world—Students explore beyond their own immediate environments.	
Recognize perspectives—Students recognize their own and others' perspectives.	
Communicate ideas—Students exchange ideas effectively with diverse audiences.	
Take action—Students translate their ideas and findings into appropriate actions to improve conditions in the world.	

*Source: Council of Chief State School Officers and Asia Society, 2010. Visit **go.solution-tree.com/specialneeds** to download and print this figure.*

Observing Co-Teaching—*Assessing Protocol*

The supplemental reading "This Doesn't Look Familiar! A Supervisor's Guide for Observing Co-Teachers" by Gloria Lodato Wilson (2005; available from Sage Journals Online, http://online.sagepub .com), will help guide and inform your team's co-teaching observations. It serves as a review of the tenets of co-teaching and will help focus your observations and discussions with your partners.

Use the template in figure 8.12 (page 136) to help plan how you and your partner might implement each of the three focus areas of the article. This "lead in" template should be used by the co-teaching team to prepare for the observation of their co-teaching implementation in the classroom. Each partner should complete the Individually, I Can column, then work together to complete the rest of the chart as a preface and guide for themselves and their observer.

The observer then uses figure 8.13 (page 136) to address a chosen few priorities in the far left column of this observation form. For each chosen concern area of the observation, the following should be noted to help the co-teaching team better understand their practice: What evidence do you see that supports the priority area? What co-teaching strategies are in place for this priority area? List any additional comments that provide clarification for both your observation and the feedback to the co-teaching partners.

Special Occasion Conversations

Figure 8.12: Adding value planning guide.

Teaching and Learning Tasks	Individually, I Can . . .	My Partner Can . . .	The Value Added Includes . . .
Meaningful roles for each teacher			
Strategies to promote success for all students			
Evidence of success			
Other concerns to observe or debrief			

*Visit **go.solution-tree.com/specialneeds** to download and print this figure.*

Figure 8.13: Value-added co-teaching observation summary.

Co-Teachers:　　　　　　　　　　　　　　School:

Grade/Subject:

Observer:　　　　　　　　　　　　　　　Date:

Observation 1 2 3 4 5 6

Meaningful Roles for Each Teacher	Evidence to Support	Co-Teaching Strategy	Comments
1. Can the role of each teacher be defined at any given point in the lesson?			
2. Is each role meaningful? Does each role enhance the learning process?			
3. Do the teachers vary their roles during the course of the lesson?			
4. Is each teacher well suited to the roles he or she is assuming?			
5. Are both teachers comfortable with process and content?			
6. Do both teachers work well with all students?			

Strategies to Promote Success for All Students	Evidence to Support	Co-Teaching Strategy	Comments
1. What evidence is there that teachers engaged in co-planning the lesson?			
2. Are the teachers focusing on process as well as content? Are they reinforcing important skills?			
3. Are the directions clear?			
4. What strategies or modifications are being employed to assist struggling students?			
5. What adaptations were made to materials in order to help struggling students complete tasks?			
6. What strategies are being used to actively engage students?			
7. How are students being grouped? Does it fit the task? Is it purposeful?			
8. What reinforcement strategies are being employed?			
Evidence of Success	**Evidence to Support**	**Co-Teaching Strategy**	**Comments**
1. Are struggling students answering or asking questions?			
2. Are students engaged in meaningful work throughout the period?			
3. How are teachers assessing the learning of each student?			
4. What evidence is there that all students have been appropriately challenged?			

Source: Wilson, G. L. (2005). This Doesn't Look Familiar! A Supervisor's Guide for Observing Co-Teachers. Intervention in School and Clinic, 40(5). *Reprinted by permission of Sage Publications. Visit* **go.solution-tree.com/specialneeds** *to download and print this figure.*

Special Occasion Conversations

IN A PERFECT WORLD CONVERSATION

Aligning With Professional Teaching Standards—*Aligning Protocol*

In order to be fully engaged in the teaching profession, many educators use the standards of their respective professional organizations as touchstones of quality.

Following are two such sets of standards. The first is from the Interstate Teacher Assessment and Support Consortium (InTASC), a consortium of state education agencies and national educational organizations dedicated to the reform of the preparation, licensing, and ongoing professional development of teachers. Created in 1987, InTASC's primary constituency is state education agencies responsible for teacher licensing, program approval, and professional development. Its work is guided by one basic premise: an effective teacher must be able to integrate content knowledge with the specific strengths and needs of students to ensure that all students learn and perform at high levels.

Their new standards (a draft for public comment) comprise a set of principles of effective teaching, critically examining what an effective teacher must know and be able to do today, and thoughtfully considering how teacher policy should change to support the vision articulated by these standards. The InTASC principles are as follows.

The Learner and Learning

Standard 1: Learner development—The teacher understands how children learn and develop, recognizing that patterns of learning and development vary individually within and across the cognitive, linguistic, social, emotional, and physical areas, and designs and implements developmentally appropriate and challenging learning experiences.

Standard 2: Learning differences—The teacher uses understanding of individual differences and diverse communities to ensure inclusive learning environments that allow each learner to reach his or her full potential.

Standard 3: Learning environments—The teacher works with learners to create environments that support individual and collaborative learning, encouraging positive social interaction, active engagement in learning, and self-motivation.

Standard 4: Content knowledge—The teacher understands the central concepts, tools of inquiry, and structures of the disciplines he or she teaches and creates learning experiences that make these aspects of the disciplines accessible and meaningful for learners.

Standard 5: Innovative applications of content—The teacher understands how to connect concepts and use differing perspectives to engage learners in critical/creative thinking and collaborative problem solving related to authentic local and global issues. (Council of Chief State School Officers [CCSSO], 2010, p. 9)

Instructional Practice

Standard 6: Assessment—The teacher understands and uses multiple methods of assessment to engage learners in their own growth, document learner progress, and inform the teacher's ongoing planning and instruction.

Standard 7: Planning for instruction—The teacher draws upon knowledge of content areas, cross-disciplinary skills, learners, the community, and pedagogy to plan instruction that supports every student in meeting rigorous learning goals.

Standard 8: Instructional strategies—The teacher understands and uses a variety of instructional strategies to encourage learners to develop deep understanding of content areas and their connections, and to build skills to access and appropriately apply information. (CCSSO, 2010, p. 10)

Professional Responsibility

Standard 9: Reflection and continuous growth—The teacher is a reflective practitioner who uses evidence to continually evaluate his or her practice, particularly the effects of his or her choices and actions on others (students, families, and other professionals in the learning community), and adapts practice to meet the needs of each learner.

Standard 10: Collaboration—The teacher collaborates with students, families, colleagues, other professionals, and community members to share responsibility for student growth and development, learning, and well-being. (CCSSO, 2010, p. 10)

While you may not be a beginning teacher, how might you and your collaborating partners use these ten InTASC standards as benchmarks in assessing your current practices and as you set new learning goals?

What other professional standards match your teaching assignment? Are there other relevant local, state, or national standards that match your interests and professionalism?

Creatively explore how your co-teaching practice can be designed to help you become more accountable to national professional standards. You might want to use the Aligning With Professional Standards Reflective Journal (fig. 8.14) to ensure that you are continually embedding the standards into your daily practice.

Figure 8.14: Aligning with professional standards reflective journal.

InTASC Standards	What We Already Do to Meet This Standard	Our Plan to Meet This Standard as Co-Teachers
The Learner and the Learning		
1. Learner development		
2. Learning differences		
3. Learning environments		

continued →

In a Perfect World Conversations

InTASC Standards	What We Already Do to Meet This Standard	Our Plan to Meet This Standard as Co-Teachers
The Learner and the Learning		
4. Content knowledge		
5. Innovative applications of content		
Instructional Practice		
6. Assessment		
7. Planning for instruction		
8. Instructional strategies		
Professional Responsibility		
9. Reflection and continuous growth		
10. Collaboration		

*Source: Council of Chief State School Officers, 2010, p. 9–10. Visit **go.solution-tree.com/specialneeds** to download and print this figure.*

CRITICAL CONVERSATIONS PROTOCOLS: SET 4—EXPAND IMPACT

9

This chapter contains the detailed conversations protocols for set 4, Expand Impact. These step-by-step activities will help you and your partner or team develop a more effective co-teaching practice. The chapter begins with focus questions and anticipated outcomes and contains three types of conversations: (1) non-negotiable, (2) special occasion, and (3) in a perfect world.

Just like in the previous three chapters, please refer to the Reflective Journal (fig. 3.1, page 46) to help you decide the best place to begin addressing the topics in this set of conversations.

Visit **go.solution-tree.com/specialneeds** to download the reproducibles for this chapter.

Focus Questions

- How can we continue to grow and develop our collaborative practice?
- Why, how, and when should we be communicating with others?
- How might we build and sustain individual and organizational capacity and support for our collaborative work?
- How can we recognize and acknowledge our successful collaborative efforts?

Anticipated Outcomes

- We have developed and implemented a standards-based professional growth plan to support our continued learning.
- We have developed and implemented a comprehensive communication plan to actively engage and nurture all necessary stakeholders.
- We have taken steps to build and sustain individual and organizational capacity by sharing expertise with others and adding to the collective wealth of our system.
- We have actively recognized and rewarded the collaborative successes we have experienced.

NON-NEGOTIABLE CONVERSATIONS

Growing Together—*Planning Protocol*

Successful partners find that developing short-term and stretch goals can guide their professional development in truly powerful ways. To continue to grow both professionally and personally, you need to be very intentional in developing plans for that growth.

Begin by asking your partner and yourself how you can continue to get better with your collaborative practice. Begin with the learning outcomes you have for your students.

Collaborate on the success indicators that will demonstrate that you are making progress to accomplish your goals.

Develop professional growth plans that will help increase the likelihood of your success. Growth plans provide a framework to help you request additional skills and tools. They can also help you improve by identifying what you want to learn more about. You might be ready to ask for new duties and responsibilities or to add new partners or teams. And don't forget to consider identifying a mentor, coach, or critical friend to ensure you continue to grow professionally and personally.

When you have a clear idea of your answers, you can begin to detail your journey toward achieving your goals using the growth plan in figure 9.1.

Figure 9.1: Growing together—planning protocol

Steps and Guiding Questions
Step 1: Identify partner/team focus/growth plan. What do we know? What do we want to learn? What do we want to be able to do?
Step 2: Describe your collective knowledge, skills, and gaps. What evidence do we have?
Step 3: Develop implementation steps. How and where will we learn? How will we build our skill level? When and how will we use the information or skills? What tasks must be done? Who is responsible for each? When will we start? Finish? What are the milestones? How will we know we are successful? How will we celebrate our successes?
Step 4: Collect and assess data. How will we know we are appropriately implementing new information or skills? To what degree is this new information producing desired student results?
Step 5: Determine assistance options. What resources might we use? What resources are available to use?

*Visit **go.solution-tree.com/specialneeds** to download and print this figure.*

Talking With Our Partners—*Communicating Protocol*

Did you ever wonder how word gets around town about what goes on in your school? Would you like to develop a strategy that ensures that your students and their families are receiving accurate information about the collaborative work you are doing rather than depending on the grapevine?

Begin a conversation with your partner to brainstorm a list of all of the stakeholders who might be affected by your collaborative efforts. Don't stop at your students and their families. Others might not be directly affected, put perhaps with some good communication early on, they might prove strong allies or provide additional resources. It is always politically smart to determine who is critical to your success and design your communications plan accordingly.

Figure 9.2 can be used as a template to help you and your partner develop your communications plan. When you are satisfied that you have answered each of the questions sufficiently, you are ready to design and implement a communications plan.

Figure 9.2: Communicating with our partners plan.

Communications Task	Who Decides?	Who Is Responsible?	By When?
What information needs to be communicated?			
Who needs to be involved?			
Who can make the best pitch?			
How do we need to get our message out?			
What hooks can we use to make sure it is well received? What connections can we make to the receiver?			
What else might we consider to be politically smart in our contacts and communications?			
Other			

*Visit **go.solution-tree.com/specialneeds** to download and print this figure.*

Building Capacity—*Sustaining Protocol*

How can we as partners ensure that our co-teaching practice is sustainable?

Michael Fullan shares the keys to successful school change in an interview (Crow, 2009). He states that this successful change is in our grasp. He's talking about whole-school reform. He says that "in terms of engagement, professional learning has to include everybody; otherwise, you only get piecemeal change" (p. 12). His ingredients for this success include:

- Developing effective leaders
- Identifying high-yield strategies

- Focusing on every child, identifying the needs of individual children, and then responding early to those needs with targeted engagement and structural improvement

- Emphasizing collaborative learning

- Leveraging entire systems

Fullan believes that everyone needs to mobilize the learning necessary to meet students' needs. He warns that the national educational emphasis remains on finding common standards, improving teacher and principal quality, using a strong data base, and focusing on the bottom tier of low performing schools. All great initiatives, but Fullan challenges that these are not capacity-building strategies; they are individualistic rather than collective strategies.

He has strong evidence to support his belief that two big things come from the collective: First, the best ideas are coordinated and therefore more focused and coherent, both vertically and horizontally. This means across grade levels and up and down the curriculum. Second, we end up with the "we-we" commitment. We stop thinking of "my students" and start thinking of "our students."

With your collaborative partners, use figure 9.3 to brainstorm all of the ways that educator conversations focus on the we-we commitment.

Figure 9.3: Educator conversations.

	I—My Kids	We-We Commitment	Suggested Strategies to Move to More Collective Commitment
Individual classrooms			
Grade level or content areas			
Schoolwide			
Districtwide			

*Visit **go.solution-tree.com/specialneeds** to download and print this figure.*

Increasing the collective is powerful. Fullan offers examples of schools that are doing so, many of them by implementing professional learning communities (PLCs). Fullan and many other experts in the field believe that PLCs have the potential for substantive, sustained leadership development. PLCs cannot assume that individuals who work in them automatically become leaders. Effective leadership development does not occur by itself. Fullan cautions that successful leadership development happens when we create environments in which developing leadership capacity coexists with school improvement efforts focused on student learning. This generative process can also be useful as you work to renew and sustain your collaborative co-teaching efforts.

How might you use your collaborative experiences to build capacity?

- Does your district have a formal leadership development plan that would foster collaborative practices?

- Is there a plan to enlist new teachers and to help others transition into collaborative opportunities?

- Do your leaders think and plan vertically and laterally?

- Is accountability provided though guiding coalitions and, if so, are those coalitions representative of collaborative efforts?

- Are leaders responsible and accountable for leadership development?

- Do you have a voice in who becomes leaders and a voice in building individual and organizational capacity?

- Who might you enlist to help with your generative possibilities?

- Are there programs or initiatives that could assist you in developing your own leadership skills?

Celebrating, Recognizing, and Acknowledging Our Successes— Reflecting Protocol

Celebrating success is a crucial part of becoming and sustaining a positive co-teaching partnership. Celebrations can communicate and reinforce what is valued in the school and can serve as a positive incentive for others. Celebrations provide the spark to sustain us in difficult times, and they have the potential to nourish our souls. Celebrations can keep our spirits high and remind us of why we do the work we do.

There are a multitude of procedures, protocols, rules, and "have tos" within every school day. One of the things we tend to overlook much too frequently is the celebration of something good that is happening. Many teachers celebrate with their students so often that their classrooms ring with joy. But even good teachers sometimes forget to stop and make the joy happen when good things happen to them and their colleagues.

How do you and your school recognize, appreciate, and acknowledge collaborative work?

With your partner, talk about the many ways that you can celebrate the collaborative efforts you have made together, either as teachers to students, as adults to adults, or individually as you have worked to improve your shared practice. Decide which of the following strategies you can implement to celebrate, recognize, and acknowledge collaborative colleagues:

- Promote your expertise! Invite people in to watch you teach, hold planning meetings, arrange observation or debriefing sessions, and conduct tuning protocols to improve your practice.

- Look for ways to share the wealth by offering to facilitate planning, problem-solving sessions, or discussions about scheduling for other teams, or to present lessons learned to faculty at meetings.

- Keep families, school administration, and school boards aware of your successes. This is the audience you will also want to ask for additional support, increased resources, or help as you move to increase individual and organizational capacity.

- Hold celebrations to honor the accomplishments of your students, and be explicit in your recognition of the added value of your co-teaching.

SPECIAL OCCASION CONVERSATIONS

Going for Maximum Impact: Putting PD Into Action—
Planning Protocol

Joyce and Showers (1995) explain multiple levels of professional impact, understanding, and application of necessary knowledge and skills. This is important to discern because many co-teachers assume that if they know the various co-teaching models, they will be effective co-teachers. We know that partners usually progress from *awareness*—meaning they can describe general concepts and identify problems and models without specifics or rationale—to a *conceptual understanding,* from which they are able to describe skills specifically with purpose and can show evidence of impact; clearly articulate concepts, models, and principles of co-teaching; and describe appropriate actions to add value through co-teaching. Conceptual understanding comes with the use of modeling and demonstrations, video, peer conversations, and so on.

Skill acquisition begins when co-teachers can begin to use the skill in structured or simulated situations, getting practice with structured conversations that guide feedback in conjunction with role plays and scenarios.

Skill application comes when partners co-teach in actual teaching situations, using various models depending on the learning goals they have agreed upon. This level of professional development impact is best acquired through coaching and supervision during actual application of co-teaching and other collaborative work. When co-teachers can coach others on a skill, we believe they are *proficient.*

These four levels of professional impact move from awareness to theory to practice. Many of the schools and educators we have worked with over the years do well with identifying a shared vision and identifying the student, adult, and practice issues; however, they jump the gun after attending a workshop that provides them with a list of models and some understanding of the issues involved. Becoming proficient as co-teachers, partners, and teams is a developmental process that moves from awareness to understanding, from acquisition of the necessary skills to application of those skills in order to move from theory into practice. While this resource can help you become aware of the knowledge, skills, and understandings to begin to experiment with co-teaching, it won't be until you are actually in practice that you are able to apply those new learnings or refine current practices to achieve mastery.

With your co-teaching partner or team, discuss how co-teaching might look at each of the levels of effective professional development.

Answer the following questions in collaboration with your partner:

1 What are we currently doing as a partnership or team to improve our co-teaching?

2 What resistance have we faced?

3 What professional development strategies have been successful and why?

4 How can we determine which levels best describe the faculty we are most likely to work with?

5 What professional development strategies would best match their needs to achieve each of these levels?

6 How can we be sure we have the necessary buy-in to support a successful professional development initiative?

Design a professional development plan for each level, using figure 9.4 as a template, that you could present to faculty members.

Figure 9.4: Going for the maximum impact: putting PD into action—planning template.

Level	Strategies We Might Employ	Target Audience
Examples		
Awareness	Basic overview presentation of collaborative teaching and co-teaching, flyers, resource list, library	School board and central office Faculty
Conceptual understanding	Study group on critical conversations	Co-teaching partners and administrators Full faculty
Skill acquisition	Workshop, webinars	Department grade-level and content teams Existing and potential co-teaching partners
Skill application	Observations, debriefs, coaching sessions	Co-teaching pairs and collaborative teams
Our Plan		
Awareness		
Conceptual understanding		
Skill acquisition		
Skill application		

*Visit **go.solution-tree.com/specialneeds** to download and print this figure.*

Taking Charge of Our Concerns—*Communicating Protocol*

Just as we differentiate our strategies to meet the needs of our diverse student population and to accommodate our collaborative partners, we might also think of the various ways we could get our message out about the work we are doing together.

Special Occasion Conversations

Whether we are sharing a successfully co-taught lesson or asking for additional resources, we will reap better rewards if we first assess the needs and readiness of our audience. There are a number of viable change process models to choose from. They all provide ways to help you understand how differently people respond when they are asked to change behaviors, values, and beliefs. Some of us jump at the change and are eager to move forward. Others are slower, but get there eventually, given the right supports and patience. Others resist and challenge district or schoolwide initiatives, causing much difficulty for partners and teams.

We have successfully used the Concerns-Based Adoption Model (CBAM), originally based on *Taking Charge of Change* (Hord, Rutherford, Huling-Austin, & Hall, 1987). CBAM offers a research-based program to help you adopt new initiatives and change processes. The premise is that if you understand where people are on a change continuum, act accordingly, know what their concerns are, and are intentional in addressing their concerns (NSDC, 2003), your change processes will be much more likely to be successful.

The best way to determine your colleagues' concerns is to listen. When we align co-teaching and collaborative practices with CBAM's seven stages of concern, we might hear the following common concerns about change for each of the stages:

1. Awareness—I'm aware of the co-teaching and collaborative efforts being introduced, but not concerned.

    + I don't really know what co-teaching is all about.

    + I don't really have an opinion, I guess. I have never collaborated in my teaching.

2. Informational—I'm interested in getting a bit more information.

    + I'm curious.

    + I'd like to hear more about this.

    + I've been starting to explore what it is all about.

3. Personal—I'm curious about the personal impact of this change.

    + What's in it for me?

    + I wanted to teach social studies; I didn't want to be a special educator.

    + What if my co-teaching partner and I don't get along?

4. Management—I'm concerned about how the change will be managed in practice.

    + Where in the world can I find the time to co-plan with someone else? I barely have time myself.

    + How can we schedule our students in general education classrooms?

    + Won't they be better off in their self-contained classroom?

5. Consequence—I'm interested in the impact on students or on the school.

    + How is this going to benefit my students?

    + What is the payoff from shared planning time, more effort, and so on?

    + Will co-teaching be worth it?

6. Collaboration—I'm interested in working with colleagues to make the change even more effective and successful.

+ I can't wait to share our collaborative efforts with the fourth-grade team.

+ I'm confident that if we can have other partnerships observe and learn from us, they will be eager to try also.

7 Refocusing—I'm interested in refining our co-teaching to improve student learning results.

+ I think if we can get more students with special needs into our general education classes, we will see our schoolwide test scores go up.

+ Our collective practice is taking on a life of its own.

+ We're starting to see so many more possibilities for co-teaching colleagues, such as other experts in the building who could help us teach and add to efforts.

+ Our co-teaching allows us to teach "in the flow"; there is a synchronicity to our collaborations.

Just as teachers try to accommodate the needs of their diverse students, change leaders must do the same. Schools generally have faculty that represent all of these seven needs when co-teaching is being presented as a new instructional strategy. When we listen to where our colleagues fall in these stages, we will be more prepared to address their concerns with the appropriate interventions, and we will know how to better deliver our messages. Interventions usually fall into the following categories: information, interest, pre-preparation, early use, and routine use. Using the concerns of others, we can be much more politically smart.

With your partner, figure out a clear and concise way to tell your story or present your request. Then scan the list in figure 9.5 (page 150) as a starting place to determine the most effective strategies to communicate your needs. Decide on the what, when, how, and by whom to make your message as powerful as possible. Examples of interventions and strategies include simply talking about your message (repeatedly, if needed); using mailbox flyers; conducting study groups, presentations, exhibits, seminars, and workshops; showcasing successes; modeling; skill building; coaching; conducting peer observations and debriefing; using reflection journals, simulations, and role plays; holding webinars; sending out emails; having public celebrations; organizing support groups; and revising or implementing policy as needed (such as curriculum and scheduling). Then record your success indicators and results.

Professionalizing Our Professional Development—
Planning Protocol

Now that you are a collaborative team, you might realize that much of the traditional professional development is neither helpful to your practice, nor linked to professional standards. How can we design the kinds of professional development activities that will actually help us grow professionally?

As partners, you have learned about one another and about your students. You now have a much clearer vision of your professional development needs. As you come up with a professional development plan, you can rely on Learning Forward to provide trusted resources and processes. Learning Forward's executive director, Stephanie Hirsh (2008), offered a plan to help administrators think about their professional development before ever deciding what they need or asking for planning time or other supports. We have modified her suggestions for your consideration as you prepare a plan and present it to your own administrators.

Special Occasion Conversations

Figure 9.5: Taking charge of our concerns.

Colleagues we hope to enlist in our collaborative change initiative	What is the best intervention or strategy to use for this potential partner?	When?	By whom?—Who is the best messenger to do this?	Success indicators—How will we know we are successful?	Results—What are the outcomes we hope for?
Teacher leadership group	Presentation of data, video clip of co-teaching, invitation to observe in classroom	Amy and Larry, special and general educators, Rebecca, EL teacher	At group's regular monthly meeting	Attentive, take us up on our offer to visit classroom Become allies to help expand our school's collaborative practices	More co-teachers; more specialists invited to co-teach with general and special educators; more kids benefiting from co-teaching

Visit go.solution-tree.com/specialneeds to download and print this figure.

Your collaborative team can use the planning template in this protocol (fig. 9.6) to help strengthen and improve the kinds of professional learning opportunities your school offers and how they are supported. You can facilitate discussions using each component on the left side of the template not only to assess your current state, but to help prioritize just how important it is to give your attention to and eventually develop action steps to address the components. These are the kinds of conversations that will ensure how you institutionalize your professional learning experiences. Because so much is at stake in doing so, we encourage you to take your time, enlist all of the necessary stakeholders, and build in an accountability process as you go.

How might you and your partner use this structure to help inform your professional development planning process?

Figure 9.6: Professionalizing our professional development.

	Current State	Improvement Priority: Low or High?	Action Plan to Address
1. Clarify purpose of professional learning for collaborative practices.			
2. Ensure learning on the job is a priority.			
3. Engage co-teachers in a process to determine the focus of professional learning.			
4. Provide co-teachers with multiple opportunities to develop deeper understanding of the content and strategies necessary to improve teaching.			
5. Give co-teachers options for how to learn content they view as essential to their students' success.			
6. Honor collaborators' experience and expertise in the planning process.			
7. Recognize and celebrate collaborators' accomplishments.			

Source: Hirsh, 2008, p. 53–54. Visit **go.solution-tree.com/specialneeds** *to download and print this figure.*

Making Our Work More Meaningful—*Planning Protocol*

To ensure successful long-term goals, it is helpful to begin with small, sure steps. Short-term goals will help you do more with what you have, make quick wins in target areas, and provide a way to begin charting your progress for the long haul.

In this activity, you will be able to use your collective intelligence and brain power to help put needed supports in place and address some of your individual learner needs.

Review the topics from figure 9.2 in the Communicating With Our Partners plan (page 143). Collaborate and come to consensus on three short-term goals for your entire team to address. Plan activities for each of the goal areas, such as the following suggested activities:

- Study groups

- Visitations to other schools

- Coaching sessions

- Aligning with other school initiatives

- Determining strategies to set up protected team time

Copy and complete the template in figure 9.7, to finish this protocol. Add your goals in the first column. Completing this activity will help to show how you and your partner might measure your success in meeting your goals by using some of these strategies. Include questions you plan to explore concerning your topics. You might want to share this plan with your entire faculty.

Figure 9.7: Making our work more meaningful protocol.

Strategies to Increase Collaboration/Co-Teaching	Brainstorm Concerns, Options, and Plans	Who Is Responsible for Follow Up?	Success Indicators

Visit **go.solution-tree.com/specialneeds** *to download and print this figure.*

Expanding Our Collaborations— *Planning Protocol*

When you and your partner are ready to expand your co-teaching efforts to others in your district, you can increase your success if you spend a little bit of time up front strategizing together to come up with a plan.

- Would an expansion of co-teaching and collaborative practices meet the needs of more students?

  + Do you have data to back up your claims that this expansion is needed?

  + Are you clear about the benefits?

  + Do you have a plan to address the challenges that are likely to arise?

- Who will participate? Determine which groups must be represented on a co-teaching/collaboration expansion team. Planning teams should ideally include about six to ten people.

- How long is our schedule? Serious long-range planning takes three months or more because of scheduling and other issues. If you have less time, scale back what you hope to accomplish. Then begin the longer-range planning for next year.

- What incentives can we offer? Why would anyone want to serve on the planning committee? The biggest incentive is the opportunity to influence programs that help students. But stipends, release time, recognition, site visits to model programs, meals, media coverage, and occasional prizes can help.

- How will we measure success? Before setting objectives, be sure your plans align with the expectations of key leaders such as the superintendent and school board members.

- Who will lead the process? Does someone in the district have the necessary skills and knowledge? Using an outside facilitator need not be expensive. Lead teachers or trainers from other nearby districts, the education service centers, or universities may be able to serve with reasonable expenses.

- Do we have the funds to support the plan?

  + Do you have funds to support the expansion process—professional development, facilitator, retreat, substitutes, and so on?

  + Do you have the necessary resources, teachers, space, scheduling options, and so on to implement the completed plan? If funds will have to be redirected, clarify that early in the process.

- Whose approval must we have? Who can veto the plan? It's critical that those who participate in planning know who holds the final power.

- Who will ensure the success of the process? Identify and cultivate key cheerleaders. Long-range planning cannot rely on the commitment and energy of one individual.

- Do we have an organizational context that supports the process?

  + Do team members trust each other and have confidence in the process?

  + Do you have the opportunity to develop awareness of learning goals and gain the buy-in of stakeholders?

Strengthening Our Support—*Sustaining Protocol*

Whether you plan to expand your co-teaching efforts or not, there will be times when you could profit from having others who support your efforts. Increasing the internal and external partners you can collaborate with will provide valuable support and resources for your practice.

Use figure 9.8 on page 154 as you and your partner brainstorm how you might think more broadly about stakeholders who could join your collaborative efforts. You might want to expand the conversations by inviting others who share a collaborative spirit or work on different team efforts, but who do not necessarily co-teach. External partners might include higher education partners, private educational consultants, and state departments of education, educational service center specialists, and resource providers and in some cases, private vendors. Internal partners might include teacher mentors, learning facilitators, classroom supports, clinical teachers, curriculum specialists, instructional specialists, data coaches, teacher leaders, and other champions of education from the community.

Figure 9.8: Strengthening our support.

	Collaboration	Co-Teaching	Consultation	Other
Who is involved?				
What services do they offer?				
What partnerships could be started or expanded?				
Who else needs to be involved in these efforts?				
To be politically smart, what else should we be thinking about?				
Who can make the best pitch?				
Other				

*Visit **go.solution-tree.com/specialneeds** to download and print this figure.*

Starting and Stopping Smartly— *Planning Protocol*

Meet with your collaborative partners before you develop your professional development goals. Brainstorm how you might first assess the kinds of training, technical assistance, coaching, and other supports designed to help improve the quality of your teaching and learning.

After listing all of the initiatives and supports, place each of them in the appropriate column on the chart in figure 9.9. If you do not have evidence to continue doing a particular initiative, it is wise to stop the initiative because it is not providing the results you want. You may find that you have gaps in what you are presently doing and will need to fill in those gaps by adding additional supports.

Figure 9.9: Starting and stopping smartly.

What are we doing now that we need to consider as we design our professional development plans?			
Continue Doing	**Stop Doing**	**Start Doing**	**Other Comments and Suggestions**

*Visit **go.solution-tree.com/specialneeds** to download and print this figure.*

IN A PERFECT WORLD CONVERSATIONS

Improving Our Expansion Efforts—*Planning Protocol*

With your partner, consider all of the ways that you might get support for your improving practice. Colleagues at a school we have worked with recently shared a report of their co-teaching committee made up of representatives who have implemented co-teaching for at least two years and were seen as experts in their building. The group met to discuss some concerns about their co-teaching practices, how they felt they were being supported, and how they might be proactive in developing an improvement plan. Following are a few of the strategies at which they arrived.

- Prior to observation visits, we will do the following:
  + With our partners, we will decide which of the improvements we've been working on we would like to have observed and what exactly we would hope to get out of our observation or debrief. We will consider what other strategies we might design to ensure that we continue to improve.

- Prior to meetings, we commit to do the following:
  + Develop written agendas of all collaboration meetings. These will be shared with our administrator and used by us to hold one another more accountable.

- During visits with collaborative coaches or experienced co-teachers, we would like the following supports:
  + Time for one-on-one discussions for co-teaching teams with the option of appointing an "outsider" colleague to serve as a mediator
  + Demonstrations of co-teaching models during instruction in the group session
  + Examples of how each model could be used in classrooms, such as types of lessons or subject matter for which it would be appropriate
  + Suggestions for equal distribution of responsibilities between the members of a co-teaching team
  + Examples of corporations that are giving support to their co-teaching program, and how the organization of those programs compares to ours in terms of success, financial support, scheduling, planning time, training, and so on
  + Facilitated discussions on the expectations of each teacher in the co-teaching team
  + Suggestions on how to handle situations where one team member isn't willing to make time to plan
  + Information about effective teaching practices and how we can apply them in our school
  + Modeling of the appropriate use of planning time
  + Suggestions for expectations for both members of co-teaching teams
  + Time for feedback on the session and input on discussion about ideas that would and would not work in our building

In a Perfect World Conversations

- Prior to observation visits, we would like the following supports:
  + A list of expectations of observations
  + The rubric that will be used as the evaluation tool
  + A schedule of the times and teams to be observed
  + A schedule of when teams will be debriefed
- During observation visits, we would like the following supports:
  + Time for debriefing for all observed teams
  + Thoughtful and clear debriefs and dissemination so that we aren't caught off guard
- During debriefing sessions, we would like the following supports:
  + Exercise or practice for evaluation of the distribution of responsibilities between the members of the co-teaching team
  + Debriefing and constructive criticism for everyone who is observed
- After observation visits, we would like the following supports:
  + Written critiques that are not a surprise because they include what was debriefed
  + Personal observations that are kept private—not distributed to all teams to read
  + A list of suggestions from which all would benefit that does not have anyone's name included

Getting Into the Policy Arena—*Sustaining Protocol*

Ingrid Carney (2010), president of Learning Forward's board of trustees, writes in the *Journal of Staff Development* that good policy enables good practice for teachers and leaders. We agree with her recommendation that effective policies at the federal, state, and local levels can ensure that job-embedded learning is a reality for us all. Only when we honor the time we need for continuous improvement and daily learning can we provide the kind of effective instruction that will ensure our students reach their potential and help them meet the global challenges they will face. She ends the column by reminding us that "well-considered policies hold great potential for promoting good practice in our schools and classrooms and making a difference for millions of American students" (p. 73).

With your partner, consider the following issues to determine if they are important enough for you to enter the realm of policymaking:

- What federal, state, and local policies currently in effect are affecting our collaborative practices?
- Are there ways that we might positively affect policies to make them more supportive of collaborative practices?
- Who are the most likely allies in our efforts to examine and improve federal, state, and local policies to improve collaborative possibilities?

Growing Our Own Teacher Leaders—*Sustaining Protocol*

Schools are finding many opportunities to use the gifts, talents, and contributions of all of the educators in their districts. One initiative that has been very successful is the concept of teacher leaders. Teacher leaders work to improve student learning in a variety of ways: they contribute to professional learning communities, model and coach continuous improvement, analyze data to stay abreast of critical trends and challenges, offer suggestions for improvements, and empower others to become involved in their efforts. Principals generally lead the charge and largely determine the success of teacher leaders.

With your partner, consider the following questions:

- What creative outlets do we need to explore to become teacher leaders?

- What leadership positions are currently available and supported in our school?

- What opportunities for training are available for those who wish to take part in teacher leadership positions?

- Are we willing to address needed changes and offer viable recommendations for improvement by becoming teacher leaders?

- Are we good listeners and also willing to facilitate tough conversations?

- Are you encouraged to take risks as you learn to be a teacher leader?

- Are you willing to invest in the growth of your colleagues?

- Are there job-embedded professional learning opportunities to help you become a more effective and efficient teacher leader?

- If you think you could be an effective teacher leader, there are two more important questions to ask yourself.

    + Why would you make a good teacher leader?

    + What are you waiting for?

Aligning With National Standards of Quality Professional Development—*Planning Protocol*

Recognizing the need for every educator to take advantage of the highest quality professional learning, Learning Forward has developed a powerful definition of professional development (Hirsch, 2009). Designed as a continuous improvement model, the definition engages educators in a cycle of analyzing data, determining student and adult learning goals, designing joint lessons that employ evidence-based strategies, providing coaching to support improvement of classroom instruction, and assessing the effectiveness of educator learning and teamwork on student learning.

Collaborative partners can use the key points of the definition to help ensure that their efforts to improve are worth the investment of time, talent, and resources. The key components call for professional learning that (1) fosters collective responsibility, (2) usually occurs several times per week, (3) adheres to a continuous cycle of improvement, (4) provides job-embedded coaching or other support to help transfer new knowledge and skills to the classroom, and finally (5) may be supported by external assistance.

In a Perfect World Conversations

Using these five key points in Learning Forward's definition of professional learning, compare the professional development efforts that are supporting your collaborative and co-teaching work using figure 9.10.

Self-reflect and then share your reflections with your partner to see how you measure up and also to help you go forward in your efforts for continuous improvement and ensure that the new knowledge and skills you gain are actually being translated into improved instruction for your students.

Figure 9.10: Professional development assessment.

Key Points of Quality Professional Learning	Current Efforts to Support Professional Learning	What We Might Put Into Place	Action Steps to Ensure Our Professional Learning Is of the Highest Quality
1. Fosters collective responsibility			
2. Occurs several times per week			
3. Adheres to continuous cycle of improvement			
4. Provides for job-embedded coaching			
5. May be supported by external assistance			

*Visit **go.solution-tree.com/specialneeds** to download and print this figure.*

AFTERWORD

Successful co-teaching partnerships that benefit students and adults begin and grow through quality conversations. Other teaching strategies and instructional methods play a part in any teaching endeavor, but teaching that draws on two or more adults in a co-teaching partnership has unique benefits for all involved. Teachers benefit from common goals, shared resources, shared responsibility, and shared accountability. Students benefit from the expertise of two or more teachers and instruction that is highly differentiated. Co-teaching is at its best when educators communicate in open dialogue with one another about the teaching and learning process. The critical conversations presented in this book give educators the foundation to reap the benefits of their collaborative relationships.

As you work through the framework and consider the complexities of learning how to work collaboratively for the benefit of your students and teaching, keep in mind the real-life stories we've presented—the stories of co-teachers that illustrate the struggles, gains, and plain hard work involved in making co-teaching beneficial for everyone. Remember Jen and Melissa who launched their school's effort to bring general education English and special education together on a daily basis for their middle school students. They started out to improve student state achievement scores, but they achieved results that were much broader and more positive than they had thought possible. The faculty and staff at Wiley School melded co-teaching into their total school structure of project-based learning to fashion their own model of what it meant to have all adults—employees and community members alike—working to help build co-teaching teams with their students. And finally, Roma and Billie built a co-teaching relationship as a cooperating teacher and a student teacher. Their relationship gave Billie a true quality mentorship and scaffolded support as a preteacher. Roma was able to give her students jointly planned lessons, instruction, and evaluation while at the same time supporting her co-teacher in learning the ropes more fully and quickly.

All of the co-teaching partnerships described in these pages are examples of ways in which professionals have come together to enhance their students' learning and their own professional development. Their critical conversations have served to enlighten and expand their growth and practice. The protocols in this book—the critical conversations to engage partners, examine data, enhance instruction, and expand impact—provide structured ways for you and your partners to enhance your dialogue and develop your professional relationship and practice for the benefit of your students.

Each group of teachers in this book found their own ways to add value to their teaching. There are as many ways to add value as there are configurations of partnerships. Just as each student you have is unique, each partnership is unique and has something special to offer. It is up to you and your partner to make it worth the effort for your students. As you grow and develop in your co-teaching, you will learn more specific ways to add value through your own practice. Until then, we offer this list of strategies:

- Develop more meaningful and productive relationships with your colleagues.

- Use and practice having quality conversations with your co-teachers often.

- Ensure successful inclusion of more students in general education classrooms.

- Build expertise in one another's specialties.

- Provide more meaningful student-teacher contact time to all students.

- Group students and lessons in creative and productive ways.

- Differentiate lessons by matching instruction with your students' interests, aptitudes, and abilities.

- Model a culture of reflection and collaboration throughout your school.

- Embed quality professional learning into your daily schedules, thereby adopting Learning Forward's purpose: *every educator engages in effective professional learning every day so every student achieves.*

- Recognize and acknowledge collaborative efforts throughout your school.

- Be good stewards of your school's investment in you as a professional.

You and your partners can apply these strategies today. There is little doubt that they require creativity, innovation, a willingness to take risks, and a commitment to teach *all* children. Needs have never been greater, resources never more scarce, and the stakes never so high. Yet it is because of these reasons that it is imperative for you and your co-teaching partners to engage in critical conversations that build your professional rapport and skills in working together.

REFERENCES AND RESOURCES

Asia Society. (2008). *Preparing our students for an interconnected world.* New York: Author.

Bartholomay, T., Wallace, T., & Mason, C. (2001). *The leadership factor: A key to effective inclusive high schools* (Grant No. H023D70102). Minneapolis, MN: Institute on Community Integration.

Bauwens, J., Hourcade, J. J., & Friend, M. (1989). Cooperative teaching: A model for general and special education integration. *Remedial and Special Education, 10*(2), 17–22.

Bouck, E. C. (2007). Co-teaching . . . not just a textbook term: Implications for practice. *Preventing School Failure, 51*(2), 46–51.

Brafman, O., & Brafman, R. (2010). *Click: The magic of instant connections.* New York: Broadway Books.

Bronson, C. E., & Dentith, A. M. (2005, November). *Facilitating effective collaborative team teaching: What instructional leaders need to know.* Paper presented at the annual convention of the University Council for Educational Administration, Nashville, TN.

Brown, J., & Isaacs, D. (2005). *The world café: Shaping our futures through conversations that matter.* San Francisco: Berrett-Koehler.

Buzbee Little, P. F. (2005). Peer coaching as a support to collaborative teaching. *Mentoring and Tutoring: Partnership in Learning, 13*(1), 83–94.

Carney, I. (2010). Good policy enables good practice for teachers and leaders. *Journal of Staff Development, 31*(6), 73.

Cole, C., Horvath, B., Sprague, J., Wilcox, B., & Pratt, C. (1999). *Quality indicators for inclusive schools: A template for including all students.* Bloomington, IN: Indiana Institute for Disability and Community.

Cole, C. M., Waldron, N., & Majd, M. (2004). Academic progress of students across inclusive and traditional settings. *Mental Retardation, 42*(2), 136–144.

Cook, L., & Friend, M. (1995). Co-teaching: Guidelines for creating effective practices. *Focus on Exceptional Children, 28*(3), 1–16.

Council of Chief State School Officers. (2010). *Interstate Teacher Assessment and Support Consortium.* Accessed at www .ccsso.org/Documents/2010/Model_Core_Teaching_Standards_DRAFT_FOR_PUBLIC_COMMENT_2010.pdf on October 20, 2010.

Council of Chief State School Officers and Asia Society. (2010). *Global competence matrix.* Accessed at www .edsteps.org/ccsso/SampleWorks/matrix.pdf on May 10, 2011.

Crow, T. (2009). Proof positive: Q&A with Michael Fullan. *Journal of Staff Development, 30*(5), 12–18.

Danielson, C. (2007). *Enhancing professional practice: A framework for teaching* (2nd ed.). Alexandria, VA: Association for Supervision and Curriculum Development.

Dieker, L. A., & Murawski, W. W. (2003). Co-teaching at the secondary level: Unique issues, current trends, and suggestions for success. *High School Journal, 86*(4), 1–13.

Drago-Severson, E. (2004). *Becoming adult learners: Principles and practices for effective development.* New York: Teachers College Press.

Drago-Severson, E. (2008). Four practices serve as pillars for adult learning. *Journal of Staff Development, 29*(4), 60–63.

DuFour, R., DuFour, R., Eaker, R., & Karhanek, G. (2004). *Whatever it takes: How professional learning communities respond when kids don't learn.* Bloomington, IN: Solution Tree Press.

DuFour, R., DuFour, R., Eaker, R., & Many, T. (2010). *Learning by doing: A handbook for professional learning communities at work*™ (2nd ed.). Bloomington, IN: Solution Tree Press.

DuFour, R., & Eaker, R. (1998). *Professional learning communities at work: Best practices for enhancing student achievement.* Bloomington, IN: Solution Tree Press.

Elmore, R. (2004). *School reform from the inside out: Policy, practice, and performance.* Cambridge, MA: Harvard Education Press.

Friend, M. (2008). *Co-teach! A handbook for creating and sustaining classroom partnerships in inclusive schools.* Greensboro, NC: Marilyn Friend.

Fuchs, D., & Fuchs, L. S. (2006). Introduction to response to intervention: What, why, and how valid is it? *Reading Research Quarterly, 41*(1), 93–99.

Fullan, M. (2001). *Leading in a culture of change.* San Francisco: Jossey-Bass.

Fullan, M. (2006). *Turnaround leadership.* San Francisco: Jossey-Bass.

Gable, R. A., Hendrickson, J. M., Evans, S. S., Frye, B., & Bryant, K. (1993). Cooperative planning for regular classroom instruction of students with disabilities. *Preventing School Failure, 37*(4), 16–20.

Garmston, R., & Wellman, B. (1999). *The adaptive school: A sourcebook for developing collaborative groups.* Norwood, MA: Christopher-Gordon.

Gately, S. E., & Gately, F. J. (2001). Understanding co-teaching components. *Teaching Exceptional Children, 33*(4), 40–47.

Hall, G. E., & Hord, S. M. (2001). *Implementing change: Patterns, principles, and potholes.* Boston: Allyn & Bacon.

Hershman, V. (n.d.). *Universal design for learning pilot program: A PATINS project statewide initiative.* Accessed at www.patinsproject.com/udl.html on September 29, 2008.

Hirsh, S. (2008). Results: Let stakeholders know what you intend to accomplish. *Journal of Staff Development, 29*(4), 53–54.

Hirsch, S. (2009). A new definition. *Journal of Staff Development, 30*(4), 10–16.

Hord, S. M., Rutherford, W. M., Huling-Austin, L., & Hall, G. E. (1987). *Taking charge of change.* Alexandria, VA: Association for Supervision and Curriculum Development.

Hutton, D. (n.d.). *Managing purposeful change: Helping people through organizational change.* Accessed at www.dhutton.com/samples/sampchang.html on October 27, 2009.

Individuals With Disabilities Education Improvement Act of 2004, Pub. L. No. 108-466, 118 Stat. 2647 (2005).

Joyce, B., & Showers, B. (1995). *Student achievement through staff development: Fundamentals of school renewal* (2nd ed.). New York: Longman.

Kahane, A. (2007). *Solving tough problems.* San Francisco: Berrett-Koehler.

King, I. C. (2003). Examining middle school inclusion classrooms through the lens of learner-centered principles. *Theory Into Practice, 42*(2), 151–158.

Kohler-Evans, P. A. (2006). Co-teaching: How to make this marriage work in front of the kids. *Education, 127*(2), 260–264.

Lambert, L. (1998). *Building leadership capacity in schools.* Alexandria, VA: Association for Supervision and Curriculum Development.

Learning Forward. (2011). [Home page.] Accessed at www.learningforward.org on March 15, 2011.

Martínez, R. S., & Nellis, L. M. (2008). Response to intervention: A school-wide approach for promoting academic wellness for all students. In B. Doll & J. Cummings (Eds.), *Transforming school mental health services: Population-based approaches to promoting the competency and wellness of children* (pp. 143–184). Thousand Oaks, CA: Corwin Press.

Marzano, R. J. (2003). *What works in schools: Translating research into action.* Alexandria, VA: Association for Supervision and Curriculum Development.

Marzano, R. J., Pickering, D. J., & Pollock, J. E. (2001). *Classroom instruction that works: Research-based strategies for increasing student achievement.* Alexandria, VA: Association for Supervision and Curriculum Development.

McLaughlin, M. W., & Talbert, J. E. (2006). *Building school-based teacher learning communities: Professional strategies to improve student achievement.* New York: Teachers College Press.

McTighe, J., & Wiggins, G. (2004). *Understanding by design professional development workbook.* Alexandria, VA: Association for Supervision and Curriculum Development

Murawski, W. W., & Hughes, C. E. (2009). Response to intervention, collaboration, and co-teaching: A logical combination for successful systemic change. *Preventing School Failure, 53*(4), 267–277.

Murawski, W. W., & Swanson, H. L. (2001). A meta-analysis of co-teaching research. *Remedial and Special Education, 22*(5), 258–267.

National Association of State Directors of Special Education. (2008). *Response to intervention: Blueprints for implementation.* Accessed at www.nasdse.org/Portals/o/DISTRICT.pdf.

National Research Center on Learning Disabilities. (2005). *Responsiveness to intervention in the SLD determination process.* Accessed at www.osepideasthatwork.org/toolkit/pdf/RTI_SLD.pdf on June 16, 2011.

National Staff Development Council. (n.d.). *NSDC's standards for staff development.* Accessed at www.learningforward.org/standards/index.cfm on September 7, 2010.

National Staff Development Council. (2003). *A measure of concern. Tools for Schools.* April/May 03, p. 1–4.

National Staff Development Council. (2010). Building global competence. *Tools for Schools. 13*(4), 1–6.

Nelson, S. W., & Guerra P. L. (2011). Cultural proficiency. *Journal of Staff Development, 32*(1), 55–56.

Nevin, A. I., Thousand, J. S., & Villa, R. A. (2009). Collaborative teaching for teacher educators: What does the research say? *Teaching and Teacher Education, 25,* 569–574.

No Child Left Behind Act of 2001, Pub. L. No. 107–110, 115 Stat. 1425 (2002).

Palmer, P. J. (1998). *The courage to teach: Exploring the inner landscape of a teacher's life.* New York: Wiley.

Palmer, P. J. (2000). *Let your life speak: Listening for the voice of vocation.* San Francisco: Jossey-Bass.

Palmer, P. J. (2004). *A hidden wholeness: The journey toward an undivided life.* San Francisco: Jossey-Bass.

PATINS Project. (n.d.) *Universal design for learning.* Accessed at www.patinsproject.com/udl on September 29, 2008.

Preddy, L. (2008). Collaboration: The Motown method. *School Library Media Activities Monthly, 25*(3), 26–28.

Rea, P. J., & Connell, J. (2005a). A guide to co-teaching. *Principal Leadership, 5*(9), 36–41.

Rea, P. J., & Connell, J. (2005b). Minding the fine points of co-teaching. *Education Digest: Essential Readings Condensed for Quick Review, 71*(1), 29–35.

Rice, D., & Zigmond, N. (2000). Co-teaching in secondary schools: Teacher reports of developments in Australian and American classrooms. *Learning Disabilities Research & Practice, 15*(4), 190–197.

Rose, D. H., & Meyer, A. (2002). *Teaching every student in the digital age: Universal design for learning.* Alexandria, VA: Association for Supervision and Curriculum Development.

Rubin, H. (2007). Through others' eyes: A collaborative model of leadership. In P. D. Houston, A. M. Blankstein, & R. W. Cole (Eds.), *Out-of-the-box leadership* (pp. 111–132). Thousand Oaks, CA: Corwin Press.

Salend, S. J., Gordon, J., & Lopez-Vona, K. (2002). Evaluating cooperative teaching teams. *Intervention in School and Clinic, 37*(4), 195–200.

Schmoker, M. (2005). No turning back: The ironclad case for professional learning communities. In R. DuFour, R. Eaker, & R. DuFour (Eds.), *On common ground: The power of professional learning communities* (pp. 135–153). Bloomington, IN: Solution Tree Press.

Scott, S. (2002). *Fierce conversations: Achieving success at work and in life, one conversation at a time.* New York: Berkeley Books.

Scruggs, T. E., Mastropieri, M. A., & McDuffie, K. A. (2007). Co-teaching in inclusive classrooms: A metasynthesis of qualitative research. *Exceptional Children, 73*(4), 392–416.

Showers, J., & Joyce, B. (1996). The evolution of peer coaching. *Educational Leadership, 53*(6), 12–16.

Sparks, D. (2007). What it means to be an outside-the-box leader. In P. D. Houston, A. M. Blankstein, & R. W. Cole (Eds.), *Out-of-the-box leadership* (pp. 11–29). Thousand Oaks, CA: Corwin Press.

Starratt, R. J. (1991). Building an ethical school: A theory for practice in educational leadership. *Educational Administration Quarterly, 27*(2), 185–202.

Starrat, R. J. (2004). *Ethical leadership.* San Francisco: Jossey-Bass.

Tan, A., & Kaufmann, U. H. (n.d.). *Making good change agents: Attitude, knowledge, skills.* Accessed at http://europe .isixsigma.com/library/content/c040501a.asp on October 27, 2009.

Thousand, J. S., Villa, R. A., & Nevin, A. I. (2007). *Differentiating instruction: Collaborative planning and teaching for universally designed learning.* Thousand Oaks, CA: Corwin Press.

Tomlinson, C. A. (2001). *How to differentiate instruction in mixed-ability classrooms* (2nd ed.). Alexandria, VA: Association for Supervision and Curriculum Development.

Tomlinson, C. A., & McTighe, J. (2006). *Integrating differentiated instruction and understanding by design: Connecting content and kids.* Alexandria, VA: Association for Supervision and Curriculum Development.

Villa, R. A., Thousand, J. S., & Nevin, A. I. (2008). *A guide to co-teaching: Practical tips for facilitating student learning* (2nd ed.). Thousand Oaks, CA: Corwin Press.

Wheatley, M. J. (2002). *Turning to one another: Simple conversations to restore hope to the future.* San Francisco: Berrett-Koehler.

Wheatley, M. J. (2005). *Finding our way: Leadership for an uncertain time.* San Francisco: Berrett-Koehler.

Wiggins, G., & McTighe, J. (2005). *Understanding by design* (2nd ed.). Alexandria, VA: Association for Supervision and Curriculum Development.

Wilson, G. L. (2005). This doesn't look familiar! A supervisor's guide for observing co-teachers. *Intervention in School and Clinic, 40*(5), 271–275.

York-Barr, J., Ghere, G., & Sommerness, J. (2007). Collaborative teaching to increase ELL student learning: A three-year urban elementary case study. *Journal of Education for Students Placed at Risk, 12*(3), 301–335.

INDEX

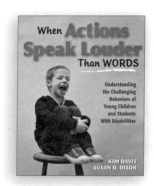

When Actions Speak Louder Than Words
Kim Davis and Susan D. Dixon
Build your understanding of behavior as communication and learn to interpret the messages behind the actions. This book provides information and tools to support all children whose primary way to communicate is through challenging behaviors.
BKF274

Differentiation and the Brain
David A. Sousa and Carol Ann Tomlinson
Examine the basic principles of differentiation in light of educational neuroscience research that will help you make the most effective curricular, instructional, and assessment choices. Learn how to implement differentiation so that it achieves the desired result of shared responsibility between teacher and student.
BKF353

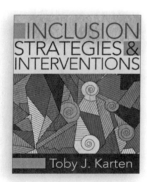

Inclusion Strategies & Interventions
Toby J. Karten
In inclusive classrooms, students with special educational needs are treated as integral members of the general education environment. Gain strategies to offer the academic, social, emotional, and behavioral benefits that allow all students to achieve their highest potential.
BKF381

Designing & Teaching Learning Goals & Objectives
Robert J. Marzano
Design and teach effective learning goals and objectives by following strategies based on the strongest research available. This first book in The Classroom Strategies Series summarizes key research behind best practices and translates that research into step-by-step hands-on strategies.
BKL001

Solution Tree | Press   a division of Solution Tree   Visit solution-tree.com or call 800.733.6786 to order.